Midship

It is 1803 and
threatening Britain
Septimus Quinn joins the Royal Navy as midshipman on the *Althea*. At once he is plunged into action, and proves in his clashes with the French that what he may lack in inches he makes up for in courage and inventiveness. Showell Styles, well known for his historical novels, has written a gripping story of adventure on the high seas, with a truly likeable hero in Septimus Quinn.

Midshipman Quinn

Showell Styles

Beaver Books

First published in 1956 by
Faber and Faber Limited
24 Russell Square, London W.C.1.
This paperback edition published in 1976 by
The Hamlyn Publishing Group Limited
London · New York · Sydney · Toronto
Astronaut House, Feltham, Middlesex, England

ISBN 0 600 36249 3

Printed in England by Cox and Wyman Limited,
London, Reading and Fakenham
Set in Intertype Baskerville
Cover illustration by John Berry

Contents

Acknowledgement

The author is indebted to Ignotus Quinn, Esquire, of Linton Abbott, for permission to use in this book various sketches and plans from the Private Log of his ancestor Septimus Quinn, whose services with the British Navy began in the year 1803, the tenth year of the struggle against Napoleon.

Chapter One

Shore Pirates

I

The smell found its way along the passages of Linton Abbott Rectory and into the study where the Reverend Theophilus Quinn was composing a sermon. The Reverend Theophilus frowned, sniffed, and addressed himself angrily to the marble bust of his second cousin, Mr William Pitt the Prime Minister, that stood on the mantelpiece.

'Drat that brat!' said the Reverend Theophilus.

The fact that his exclamation sounded like part of a child's spelling-book made him angrier still. He got up from his desk, a large pompous man in a white wig and black knee-breeches, and tugged the bell-rope that hung in a corner of the study. In a few moments a spotless frilled cap poked itself into the room and the plump body of Mrs Cattermole the housekeeper followed it. The Rector of Linton Abbott, who had been pacing up and down the study, turned to face her.

'Mrs Cattermole,' he observed solemnly, 'there is a smell in this house. I fancy—'

'A stink I'd call it, begging your pardon!' interrupted the housekeeper sharply. 'It's that lad again, I'll warrant – your nephew, sir. And, sir, I'm the camel!'

'The – the camel, Mrs Cattermole?' repeated the Rector, raising one elegant white hand in surprise.

Mrs Cattermole twisted her hands excitedly in her apron.

'The camel as the last straw broke the back of, sir!' she asserted loudly. 'Ever since your poor brother Mr Charles's boy came to live here we've had naught but noises and stinks and contraptions. There's that monster Bonaparte waiting on t'other side of the Channel to come across and murder us all in our beds, but I declare young Master Septimus is worse than the French!'

'Yes, yes, Mrs Cattermole,' nodded the Reverend Theophilus, waving his hands rather helplessly. 'I – ah – rang for you to ask you to go up to Master Septimus's room and request him—'

But Mrs Cattermole was determined to have her say now that she had started.

'Worse, I said, and I meant worse!' she continued. 'We've got our brave Nelson to deal with Napoleon and his French rascals, but who's to deal with Septimus Quinn, I'd like to know? I've just got all my rooms washed down and smelling sweet of lavender, and now comes a nasty stink like—'

'Allow me to speak, ma'am, if you please!' The Rector at last succeeded in stemming the flood of words. 'You ask who is to – ah – deal with Master Septimus. That problem, Mrs Cattermole, will shortly be solved – very shortly.'

'And glad to hear it I am, sir,' said the housekeeper, nodding her frilled cap violently. 'Twenty years I've kept house for you, and I've no wish to leave, I assure you. But to stay here with Master Septimus up to tricks of all sorts, not that he's a bad boy, only queer-like in his ways, having no brothers or sisters I daresay it is – well, he's too much to look after, and that's gospel, sir.'

The Rector seated himself somewhat wearily at his desk.

'When my brother died last year leaving his only son parentless, Mrs Cattermole,' he said, 'arrangements had already been made for the boy's future. I merely undertook to give him a home until such time as those arrangements came into effect. I have been expecting, for some days now, the arrival of a certain person who will put an end to my responsibilities, and to your – ah – troubles, as far as Master Septimus is concerned.'

'Indeed, sir.' Mrs Cattermole looked at him sharply and her voice took on a different tone. 'You don't mean as you've sent for a tutor, sir, or some harsh personage to look after that poor lamb?

I'm sure poor dear Master Septimus means no harm! Just forget my tantrums, sir, and don't bring into this house any—'

'No, no, no, Mrs Cattermole!' broke in the Reverend Theophilus distractedly. 'You mistake my meaning. The person I expect is merely the messenger who will bring the order for Master Septimus to—'

Slam-bang!

A muffled double report cut him short.

'Mercy on us – cannon!' cried Mrs Cattermole.

'Drat him!' cried the Reverend Theophilus loudly, springing to his feet and hurrying out of the room.

The housekeeper, her round face expressing the shock she felt at hearing the Rector use such a word, followed him upstairs. The acrid smell grew stronger as they climbed, and was particularly strong on the landing. In fact, some wisps of bluish smoke, which seemed to be the cause of the smell, were curling out from under a door at the head of the stairs. There was a neat notice pinned to the door. It said:

BUSY
NOCK TWICE

The Rector's impulse was to burst into the room at once, but experience of his nephew's arrangements made him more prudent. He 'nocked' twice urgently. At once the door opened as though by some magic agency, letting out a concentrated waft of the smell which had previously annoyed them. The Reverend Theophilus clapped his handkerchief over his nose.

'Septibus!' he roared. 'Cub here ibbediately!'

A small figure standing by a littered table at the far end of the room turned calmly at the words, loosing the cord which by a neat arrangement of pulleys and loops had released the catch of the door.

'Yes, Uncle,' said Septimus Quinn obediently.

But it was typical of him that he went first to the window and threw it wide open to allow the fumes to escape. He was fifteen years of age but looked less because of his lack of height. He wore a pair of large steel-rimmed spectacles and his black hair was cut shorter than was the fashion of 1803, but the general effect of neatness was spoiled by a large black smudge which covered most of the lower half of his small pale face.

'Are you killed, my lamb?' demanded Mrs Cattermole shrilly as he approached.

'Pray don't distress yourself, ma'am,' returned Septimus gravely. 'I am alive.'

'And what was the cause of that – ah – explosion?' inquired the Rector sternly.

Septimus unhooked his spectacles and turned to his uncle with the air of a lecturer explaining something simply for the benefit of his audience.

'A little experiment, sir,' he replied courteously. 'It had occurred to me that if the substance known as Potassium Chlorate were to be contained in some small vessel with the right quantity of Sulphur, and the compound impacted – that is to say, if I hit it a pretty fair whack with a pestle – the result would be an expl—'

'Enough!' thundered the Reverend Theophilus, pointing to a door on the landing. 'You will wash your face, sir, and then come to my study. I wish to have a talk with you.'

Three minutes later Septimus Quinn presented himself in his uncle's study. He was washed and tidy but otherwise not perceptibly subdued. Indeed, as Mrs Cattermole had discovered, it was practically impossible to subdue Septimus Quinn. The only sign that he was anticipating trouble was the fact that he was still wearing his steel-rimmed spectacles. Septimus had no real need of spectacles in the ordinary way, and wore them chiefly for reading or close work; he was exceptionally long-sighted, and could follow the lofty flight of a skylark long after most people had lost sight of it. But he had a habit of carrying them about with him and putting them on whenever he was confronted with a problem. He said it helped him to think better.

The Reverend Theophilus was annoyed by this habit; it made his nephew look too old and wise for his years.

'Take those things off, boy,' he snapped irritably, 'and sit down there.'

'Very well, Uncle,' said Septimus, obeying.

The Rector frowned at him in silence for a few moments. He was not an unkind man, but he found it quite impossible to understand Septimus. In the days when the Reverend Theophilus was young, boys had been boys. They ran races, played games, gave each other black eyes and gory noses, and never looked inside a book unless they had to. Septimus was quite different. He read every book he could lay hands on and seemed to be more interested in how a football was made than in kicking it. And he was for ever experimenting. Not for the first time, the Rector wondered what on earth would happen to Septimus when he was plunged into the career he was destined to follow.

'My boy,' he said gravely, 'I feel I am to blame. I should have had this talk with you long ago. I fear I have been too much occupied with my own work to give you the care I should have given.'

'Pray don't distress yourself, Uncle,' replied Septimus with equal gravity. 'You have been exceedingly kind.'

It was one of Septimus's most irritating habits to tell people not to distress themselves, and the Reverend Theophilus felt some of his kindness evaporating.

'I cannot understand you,' he went on rather more sharply than before. 'For more than a year you have known what your career is to be. For the last two months you must have realised that any day might see you summoned to take your place in that calling. Yet what steps have you taken to prepare yourself for it?'

Septimus continued to regard him calmly in silence. He knew by now that his uncle required no reply to questions of this kind.

'Your activities during the time you have resided here,' pursued the Rector, 'have been remarkable only for their – ah – peculiarity. At present your time, and the pocket-money which your father directed should be paid to you, appear to be devoted to playing about with dangerous chemicals.'

'Not dangerous, Uncle,' observed Septimus mildly. 'I took care to read Doctor Priestley's manual—'

'Do not interrupt me. Before that, you employed your leisure in acquiring the art of glass-blowing, in the course of which this house was twice nearly set on fire. Before that again, it was carpentry – a menial occupation for one of your birth. There was the disgraceful occasion – I trust you have not forgotten it, for I have not – when you went about this village and countryside in a succession of disguises, including' – the Reverend Theophilus snorted disgustedly – 'including the disguise of a travelling juggler.'

'It took a long time to learn all those tricks,' nodded Septimus thoughtfully.

'Bah! What use will they be to you? And where was your dignity, sir? You seem to have no conception of what will be required of you in the near future, and it is my duty as your guardian – a duty which, perhaps, I have neglected – to enlighten you.' The Rector placed the tips of his fingers together and settled himself in his chair. 'I shall begin by drawing your attention to the perilous situation in which Britain finds herself at this time.'

Septimus perceived that he was in for a long lecture. It was characteristic of him that he did not fidget or shuffle his feet. He was capable of remaining perfectly still for long periods; indeed, he had once tested himself, by way of experiment, and had succeeded in standing motionless for two hours and a quarter outside the Rectory toolshed.

'This country,' began the Reverend Theophilus, 'has been fighting the French for ten years. I do not count the few months of uneasy peace which ended last May. Napoleon Bonaparte has sworn to bring all Europe under his rule, and he has succeeded with every nation except one. Britain alone remains to defy him. At this moment a huge invasion army is gathered on the other side of the Channel, waiting to attack. In his armies Bonaparte has ten men to our one. You perceive that this country and people –

including you and I, Septimus – are in the greatest danger.'

He paused. Septimus knew all this well enough, but he went on listening politely with one ear. The other was cocked to listen to a sound from outside, the sound of cantering hooves approaching the Rectory; they seemed to have turned into the gate and now clattered to a standstill at the door.

'One thing only,' resumed the Rector, 'stands between Britain and her terrible foe – the British Navy. By God's grace our seamen and sea-officers are the finest the world has ever seen. That, Septimus, is why I am wondering how you, when the time comes, will—' He broke off as the housekeeper, after knocking at the study door, came in. 'Well, Mrs Cattermole?'

'The mail rider from Petersfield just brought this, sir,' said Mrs Cattermole, holding out a flat oblong package. 'It's addressed to Master Septimus and marked "Urgent", so thinking as perhaps I'd best bring it straight in—'

'Thank you, Mrs Cattermole.'

The Reverend Theophilus took the package and waited until she had gone out. Then he glanced at the heavy seal, imprinted on purple wax.

'I do believe,' he said in some agitation, 'that my instructive talk has come too late after all.'

'As the package is addressed to me, Uncle, I'd better open it,' suggested Septimus.

'Of course, my boy, of course.'

Septimus slit the covering and took out a folded sheet of stiff paper. As he read its contents his small face gave no hint of the excitement he felt. At last he looked up.

'It's from the Admiralty in London, Uncle,' he said calmly. 'It says that Mr Septimus Quinn, hitherto borne on the books of His Majesty's ship *Centurion*, is transferred as Midshipman to His Majesty's frigate *Althea* – and is to report on board for immediate duty.'

2

'Ar,' said old Lambie the carrier, flicking his whiplash at the ear of his aged horse as they clattered along the dusty lanes. 'So you be away off to fight they Frenchies in a King's ship. Ar.'

'In a frigate, Lambie, not a battleship,' corrected Septimus.

'Ar,' said Lambie. 'Well, you be mortal young, Master Sep. But Lord Nelson, he were younger nor you when he jined as a midshipman, so you keep a-goin' and mebbe you'll end up a lord.'

The carrier's cart was bearing Mr Midshipman Quinn to Petersfield, where he would get the Portsmouth coach. It was a sunny morning towards the end of July, two days after the arrival of the letter from the Admiralty.

Those two days had been busy ones at Linton Abbott Rectory. Septimus had to be outfitted for his new career, and only the fact that the tailor at Alton was Mrs Cattermole's brother-in-law had enabled two blue coats of regulation pattern to be completed in the time. The white breeches and stockings and buckled shoes Septimus already possessed. A retired naval lieutenant with a wooden leg, who lived in the parish, had advised as to the cut of the coats and the style of cocked hat to be worn, and had even given Septimus the dirk he had worn as a midshipman. Septimus himself had constructed the small but stout sea-chest, with his name on it, which was now stowed behind him in the carrier's van. He was fully equipped with everything – except knowledge of ships and the sea.

Before he died, Mr Charles Quinn had contrived to have his son's name placed on the books of one of His Majesty's ships as a midshipman, which privilege he was able to obtain without difficulty because of his distant relationship to William Pitt, now Prime Minister of England. It was quite a common arrangement for this to be done, and it gave extra seniority; Septimus Quinn would have over a year's seniority as midshipman before he even set foot on board a ship. But though boys were sometimes 'borne 'on the books' for years, often while they were still at school, without being appointed to a seagoing ship, in time of war they were likely to be called up at very short notice. And this had happened to Septimus.

As the carrier's cart rumbled through Selborne and out into the sunlit lanes towards Greatham, Septimus Quinn had every reason for feeling unsettled and anxious about his future. He was not, in his own opinion, a fighter. The only boat he had ever been in was an ancient punt on a lake near Linton Abbott. Yet here he was, setting forth to go to sea in a fighting frigate with two hundred shipmates who were all strangers to him. But Septimus, it will have been noticed, was of a philosophical turn of mind. With no brothers and sisters, and – after his father's death – no real friends, he had learned to be self-sufficient and independent. He had also developed a knack of being interested in everything that came his way and finding out what he could about it, whether it was a lump of sulphur or a gypsy conjuror. So in spite of the perils and adventures that undoubtedly lay ahead of him he was neither afraid nor particularly excited. On the whole, he would have preferred to stay at Linton Abbott and do some more research into the remarkable properties of Potassium Chlorate when united with Sulphur; but he was prepared to be interested in fighting the French now that it was to be his profession.

'See them there?' demanded old Lambie suddenly, pointing with his whip to a small company of men marching raggedly across a field beside the lane. 'Volunteers, they calls 'em. Drilling to fight Boney if he crosses the Channel, they are. Volunteers! Ar!' He spat to show his opinion of them. 'Rapscallions, I calls 'em!'

'Why so?' asked Septimus politely.

'Why? 'Cause half on 'em's thieves and vagabonds what's jined for the bounty they pays, two golden guineas! Most on 'em desert when they've got the money and turns thief or footpad. I tell ee, Master Sep, there's been coaches stopped, and that not far from here, by those gentry!'

'Highwaymen, you mean.'

'Ar. Cummup!' Lambie flicked his whip at his old horse. 'Last week the Lunnon coach were stopped, Guildford way. Wouldn't surprise me if they black rascals tried their tricks on me some day. Ar!'

'Would you fight if they stopped you?' asked Septimus.

'Who – me? That I wouldn't!' said Lambie emphatically. 'And if ever you're in a coach what's held at pistol's point by they toby-men, Master Sep, you sit quiet and do as they tell you. That's my advice. 'Tis a hanging matter to stop a coach on the King's highway, so if they have to shoot they shoot to kill. Ar!'

'I don't think I'd like to sit quiet in those circumstances,' remarked Septimus thoughtfully.

'No – and you'd not like to lie quiet with a pistol-bullet in you, neither! Cummup!'

There was a very bumpy piece of road just before they rattled into Greatham, and as the cart lurched into one particularly deep hole Septimus was flung with some force against the rail at the side of his seat. He thrust his hand into his coat-pocket just in time to prevent the thing that lay there from being crushed.

'Hallo!' said Lambie. 'Carrying eggs in your pocket, Master Sep?'

'One egg, Lambie,' replied Septimus solemnly. 'And it's a glass one, too.'

The carrier guffawed at what he thought was a joke. But the thing in Septimus's pocket was indeed made of glass, and about the size and shape of a pigeon's egg. Septimus had made it himself the previous evening. It represented a further stage in his chemical experiments, and he was hoping to test it when he got a moment to himself.

Lambie, who was a simple soul, chuckled over the 'glass egg' joke all the way to Petersfield and was still chuckling when he pulled up outside the Red Lion Inn. Petersfield was on the main London-to-Portsmouth road twenty miles from Portsmouth – two hours' going for the London Mail coach. Lambie helped Septimus to get his sea-chest into the porch of the inn and then bade him farewell.

'London coach'll be here in an hour, if she's up to time,' he said.

'Your uncle told me he'd an inside place reserved for you. So you've time for filling your belly, Master Sep – and my advice is, fill it well. You'll have nowt but salt beef and rotting biscuits once you go to sea!'

Septimus shook hands with him and then went into the inn.

It must be admitted that he felt, for the first time, rather lonely; old Lambie the carrier was the last link with Linton Abbott Rectory and the Reverend Theophilus and Mrs Cattermole – with Home. But no one would have suspected that the small figure in white breeches and blue coat who entered the coffee-room so confidently was feeling anything but perfectly calm. There were several people in the raftered coffee-room, eating at the long table in the window. Septimus took a vacant chair and, when he had ordered the 'ordinary' dinner from the waiter, turned his gaze on his companions. There were two men who looked like farmers, eating steak-pudding noisily; a well-dressed lady in cloak and bonnet, with her daughter, a pretty girl of about Septimus's age; and, at the end of the table opposite Septimus, a tall, bony gentleman with a red face and bulging blue eyes, clad like Septimus in white breeches and blue uniform coat but with a great deal of gold braid on his coat-sleeves. It hardly needed the straight sword and cocked hat lying on the window-seat to tell Septimus that this was a real naval officer.

The old wooden-legged lieutenant at Linton Abbott was the nearest approach to a sea-officer of the British Fleet that Septimus had ever seen, and it is possible that his steady grey eyes remained fixed on the red-faced officer rather longer than was polite. It soon appeared that the officer thought so.

'Hah!' he said suddenly glaring back at Septimus. 'Don't think I've the honour of your acquaintance, sir!'

His voice was like the rasping of a file a thousand times magnified, thought Septimus.

'No, sir,' he admitted.

'But by Hector, you're determined to know me when we meet again!' rasped the officer. 'Hah! Hah-hah-hah!'

He appeared to think that he had made a particularly good joke. Septimus observed that the girl was smiling, and decided that he didn't like the red-faced gentleman.

'Hah-hah-hah!' he responded.

On the face of it, he seemed to be politely joining in the laugh. But in Septimus's laughter there was just the suspicion of an echo of the red-faced officer's horse-laugh – faint indeed, but enough to make that gentleman go a deeper red and glare wrathfully, while the girl buried a fit of giggles in her handkerchief. Perhaps fortunately, the waiter provided a diversion by arriving at that moment with a plate of steak-pudding for Septimus, and the meal proceeded in a silence broken only by the lusty gobbling of the two farmers.

Septimus, remembering Lambie's advice, dealt heartily with the Red Lion's excellent pudding. As he ate he reflected with satisfaction that he had not altogether lost the accomplishment of mimicry. Six months ago one of his peculiar studies had been the imitation of the voice of every bird and beast, and most of the human inhabitants, of Linton Abbott.

Presently the red-faced officer got up, and with a final glare at Septimus went into the taproom, where he could be heard shouting ill-temperedly for wine. A little later the landlord of the Red Lion came into the coffee-room.

'Ladies and gents,' he said, wiping his hands on his apron, 'by your leave, London coach is doo in ten minutes.'

'Landlord!' called the lady, as he was turning to go. 'A word with you— Is it true that mail coaches have been robbed on the Portsmouth road lately?'

'We-e-ell,' replied the landlord hesitatingly, 'it's true there's been a bit of trouble, now and again, with the toby-men. But you've no call to be afeard, ma'am,' he added quickly. 'The guards on all the London Mails is armed with blunderbusses, since last Toosday. What's more, you'll be safe in Portsmouth by six o'clock in the evening and them rascals don't usually pull their flash tricks by full daylight.'

'Thank you,' said the lady. 'I am not afraid, I assure you.

Particularly,' she added, with a pleasant smile at Septimus, 'as we have a King's officer with us. I presume, sir, you are travelling to Portsmouth?'

Septimus rose from his chair. 'I am, ma'am,' he returned.

'I am Lady Barry, and this is my daughter Philippa.'

'My name is Septimus Quinn,' said Septimus, and only just remembered to add, 'Midshipman.'

He made his best bow, Lady Barry inclined her head graciously, and Philippa dropped a curtsey.

'We must see to our baggage,' said Lady Barry. 'Come, Philippa. No doubt we shall meet on the coach, Mr Quinn.'

They went out of the coffee-room. Septimus paid for his dinner and went to move his sea-chest outside ready for the coming of the coach. The sunshine of morning had gone, and the sky was covered with dark clouds. Septimus had been wishing that his place on the coach had been an 'outside', but now he felt he was fortunate. If it was going to rain, the top of a coach was an uncomfortable place to be for a two-hour journey.

The two farmers came out of the inn and walked away after a gloomy glance at the sky; evidently they were not travelling by the coach. Septimus's eye was caught by a handbill stuck on the wall of the inn. The print was small and blurred, and to read it more easily he got his steel-rimmed spectacles out of his pocket and put them on. The notice was headed 100 GUINEAS REWARD! and offered that amount for the apprehension of 'a Highway Thief or Toby-Man styling himself Jeremy Craw,' who had held up a coach near Richmond some weeks before. As he was reading it a step sounded behind him and a harsh voice spoke.

'Hah! Thinking of catching this shore pirate, I presume?'

Septimus straightened up and looked round. The red-faced officer was looking at him as if he was a particularly loathsome insect.

'Good gad!' he exclaimed in mock horror. 'Spectacles! A spectacled midshipman – never heard of such a thing, by Hector! Hah! Anyone'd mistake you for a learned man!'

Septimus appeared to consider the point for a moment. 'They

might mistake me for one,' he admitted; and there was a faint but distinct emphasis on the 'me'.

The red-faced man stiffened and his protruding blue eyes sparkled angrily.

'See here, my lad!' he barked, and now there was a threatening ring in his voice. 'You'll address me as "sir" and you'll lift your hat when you speak. Understand? If I couldn't see with half an eye that you're an ignorant young lubber who's never been to sea, I'd report you to your captain, whoever he may be! Now then, do as I order you – salute!'

Septimus saw that he had the worst of it this time. He lifted his cocked hat without any trace of impudence. 'Yes – sir!' he said.

'Hah!' snorted the officer, 'When you're out of baby-clothes you'll learn that we say *aye aye* in the Navy, not *yes, sir* like a confounded waiter. Remember Lieutenant Pyke told you that. Hah!'

With a final snort he stalked away. It occurred to Septimus that his first contact with a real sea-officer had not been very encouraging; and he disliked Lieutenant Pyke more than ever. Still, he told himself, the officers of H.M. frigate *Althea* would probably be less unpleasant. At that moment a thunder of wheels and hooves came to his ears, rapidly approaching, and the clear notes of a bugle-horn rang in Petersfield High Street. The *Highflyer* mailcoach dashed up in fine style and pulled up before the Red Lion with its four horses panting and sweating.

'Five minutes honly!' bellowed the guard, jumping down from his high seat at the back – Septimus noted the blunderbuss in its big leather holster strapped there. 'Mount all, hif you please!'

Exactly five minutes later the *Highflyer* clattered away on the last stage of its journey to Portsmouth. There were five passengers travelling 'inside': Lady Barry, her daughter, and Mr Midshipman Quinn occupied one seat, and facing them were Lieutenant Pyke and a lean man in a brown travelling-coat who appeared to be asleep with his hat pulled over his eyes.

3

The *Highflyer* had not gone more than a mile along the Portsmouth road when rain began to fall heavily. Lieutenant Pyke asked Lady Barry if she would like the coach window pulled up, and introduced himself.

'Lady Barry?' he repeated when she informed him of her own name. 'Can it be that you're the mother of Midshipman Charles Barry? Then by Hector – if you'll pardon me, my lady – your son and myself are shipmates!'

'Indeed!' replied Lady Barry without much enthusiasm. 'You, sir, are of course the Lieutenant George Pyke of whom Charles has told me.'

'Your ladyship's most obedient servant!' Pyke was all smiles. 'Delighted to make your ladyship's acquaintance. Hah!'

'Do you think, sir,' asked Lady Barry, 'that the coach will be late arriving at Portsmouth?'

'If she can keep up this rate of knots, ma'am – no. But I fear the rain will make the roads heavy. However, speaking of your son Charles, ma'am, I think him a fine young fellow. If all the midshipmen of His Majesty's Navy were as active and zealous' – here Septimus detected a scornful glance in his direction – 'we should have no trouble in finding first-rate officers. Yes, ma'am, I find Charles Barry the very example of what a young gentleman—'

At this point Mr Midshipman Quinn ceased to follow the conversation. The air in the coach had grown stuffy, and he began to feel as sleepy as Philippa Barry, who was already dozing in her seat beside him. Before he sank into uneasy slumber, however, Septimus happened to glance at the lean man in the brown travelling-coat, who was still motionless and silent in the corner. The man was not, as he seemed to be, asleep. Beneath the brim of his low-crowned hat one very bright black eye kept ceaseless watch out of the window.

That gleaming black eye seemed to flit in and out of Septimus

Quinn's dreams, and always it was somehow linked with the name of Jeremy Craw the highwayman. Once, when Septimus half-awoke, it was to find that the *Highflyer* was no longer speeding at a rocking canter through the rain but going at a slower pace; evidently they had reached the place where the road began to

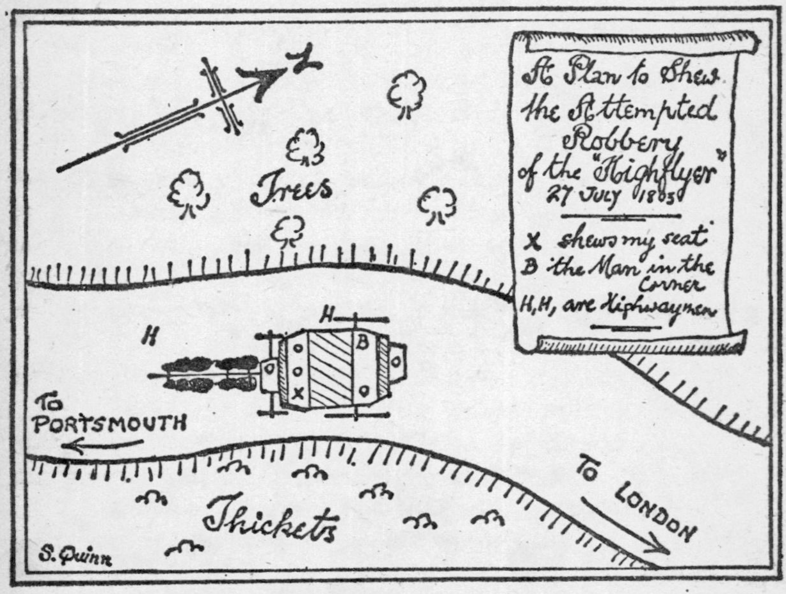

The first drawing in Midshipman Quinn's Log

climb through the gap of the South Downs before dipping and rising again to begin the last descent through Horndean to Portsmouth. The coach windows were steamed up, but someone had rubbed a patch of glass clear, and through it could be seen the thin rain and a dank white mist which it had raised from the warmer ground. Septimus slid back into sleep again.

He woke with a jerk. The coach was jolting to a sudden standstill. Men's voices yelled outside in the rain.

'Get clear, there!'

'Stand! Stand and deliver!'

'Here's for you, you—'

'Don't touch that gun, or—'

Above the sound of trampling hooves came the heavy report of a pistol, followed instantly by a groan and a thud from the coach roof.

Inside the coach there was consternation. Lady Barry stifled a shriek and clutched her daughter to her. Lieutenant Pyke, rasping out an oath, stumbled to his feet and tried to get his sword from its place on the rack above his head. Septimus, from force of habit, groped in his pocket for his spectacles but was now awake enough to realise that this was not the time to wear them. His fingers touched the 'glass egg' that lay there. As for the lean man in the corner, he was sitting bolt upright and his little eyes were very bright.

'Everyone will please keep their places,' he said commandingly; and his right hand held a short-barrelled pistol. 'This coach has been stopped by highwaymen—'

'And you're an accomplice, by Hector!' roared Lieutenant Pyke, and flung himself bodily upon the lean man.

Lady Barry shrieked in earnest, Pyke bellowed angrily, the lean man struggled and tried to shout something. Septimus caught a word or two. 'Fool! . . . Bow Street . . . Jeremy Craw . . .'

And then the window flew down with a bang. In the square opening appeared a face – or part of a face. The grinning mouth was plain to see, but the upper half of the face was covered with a black mask through which hard grey eyes gleamed dangerously. A long pistol slid into view and rested on the sill, its muzzle slowly moving to point at each occupant of the coach in turn.

'I'll shoot if there's any tricks!' warned the highwayman sharply. 'And if I shoot,' he added grimly, 'you'll be dead mutton – same as the guard!' His eyes fell upon Pyke and the lean man, who had disentangled themselves and were glaring at each other. 'Well, well, well!' he chuckled. 'If it isn't Mr Prince of the Bow Street Runners!'

'It is,' said the lean man between his teeth. 'And if it hadn't been for this – this porpoise here, I'd have taken you, Jeremy Craw!'

'Better luck next time, Mr Prince,' grinned Craw. 'Let's hope the naval porpoise is less of a fool at sea than he is ashore.

During this exchange Septimus had been cautiously peering to see what had become of Mr Prince's pistol. As the highwayman finished speaking he spotted it. In the struggle with Pyke it had been dropped on the floor of the coach amongst the straw. Septimus was planning to edge it towards himself with his foot when Jeremy Craw's glance fell on it.

'Pick that up and give it to me!' he snapped. 'Not you, Prince – the girl yonder! Quickly!'

Philippa Barry gave a little shudder and then bent to pick up the pistol. Septimus saw a sudden light flame in her eyes. She grabbed the pistol, levelled it swiftly at Craw – and screamed as his grip fastened on her wrist.

'Little vixen!' he snarled. 'You'd bite, would you?' He dropped the pistol into his pocket. 'You'd have done no harm if you'd pulled trigger – it wasn't cocked. But any more tricks and I'll mark your pretty face for life!'

'By Hector!' roared Pyke, purple in the face. 'Would you hurt women, you – you shark?'

'I'll hurt anyone who tries to hurt me. Get into that corner, porpoise – right back where I can see you. Now then.'

Jeremy Craw wrenched open the door of the coach and stood with one booted foot on the step, his pistol swinging to cover the five in the coach. Behind him Septimus could see the roadside trees looming dimly through a steamy mist, and a saddled horse cropping the grass.

'Listen here!' snapped Craw. 'I'm a toby-man with no time to waste. I've had to shoot the guard and I've got my pal covering the coachman. I want everything you've got in your pockets – and you two females can take off your jewels and rings. No dallying, see? First to make a false move gets a bullet and I'll use the butt on the next.'

'You'll swing for this!' gobbled Pyke, shaking with wrath.

'Not on your account, my fancy-man! No more talking – fork out! Mr Prince, I'll thank you to clasp your hands on top of your empty head, where I can see 'em. That's it.' He turned to Lady Barry. 'You first, madam. Hand over everything, and no harm'll come to you. Keep anything back – and I'll search you. See?'

'I will give you everything I have,' said Lady Barry coldly. She took off a necklace, a bracelet, and three rings, and placed them in the highwayman's outstretched palm with her purse. Philippa, her face pale but composed, contributed a little purse and a bracelet. Jeremy Craw looked beyond her at Septimus, who had scarcely moved a muscle since the coach had stopped.

'You boy, there!' he barked, grinning unpleasantly. 'You infant in fancy-dress – not dead, are you? Hand over! Money and any other little things you've got!'

'I – I have got a little thing here,' faltered Septimus in a childish voice.

His fingers were in his pocket, closing round the 'glass egg'. It flashed through his mind that as an opportunity for testing it this occasion was unique. His hand came out of his pocket slowly, and then flicked like a lash of a whip. The glass egg flew straight and true for the centre of the black mask. There was a deafening bang, a screech from the highwayman, a whirl of acrid smoke, a fierce cry from Mr Prince.

Septimus, who had flung himself forward as the home-made bombshell burst, saw through the smoke that Prince had gripped the toby-man's pistol arm and was forcing it down. The pistol fell from the man's hand and simultaneously Craw broke free. Septimus pounced on the fallen pistol and levelled it as the highwayman ran unsteadily for his horse. Jeremy Craw was barely five paces away when Septimus pulled the trigger. The bullet struck high, below the left shoulder, and the highwayman, flinging his arms wide, fell sprawling into the mud of the roadway and lay still.

Septimus and Mr Prince sprang from the coach together – in time to see a dim figure galloping away into the mist. Jeremy Craw's 'pal' had not waited to see the fate of his leader. The Bow Street Runner bent over the fallen toby-man for a moment and then straightened up.

'All's fine,' he said with satisfaction. 'He'll live to be strung up at Tyburn.'

'The credit is to this young gentleman,' said the voice of Lady Barry; she had dismounted from the coach, with Philippa. 'If it had not been for him—'

'Without Mr Prince's quick action, ma'am,' Septimus put in swiftly, 'my efforts wouldn't have been much use.'

'All the same,' said Mr Prince, 'you did the trick, sir. I'll see to it that you get a proportion of the reward in due course. But I'd like to know what was in that thing you threw.'

'The substance known as Potassium Chlorate,' began Septimus, 'enclosed with a certain amount of Sulphur in a glass container—'

A hoarse voice from above their heads interrupted him.

'Ladies and sirs,' it said, 'my guard's been shot dead, pore feller, and that's bad. A celebrated 'ighwayman's been took, and that's good. But good or bad, this 'ere coach 'as got to get to Portsmouth as quick as maybe.'

They looked up to see the coachman's round face, somewhat pale after his fright, looking anxiously down at them. Mr Prince nodded in a business-like fashion.

'Quite right,' he said. 'I had better explain, my lady, that I'm Dennis Prince of Bow Street, and it's my trade to run down rogues like this Jeremy Craw. I shall take charge of him from now on. And since his wound's not likely to keep him unconscious for long, I shall ask the Lieutenant to help me tie him up. There's rope in the boot of the coach.'

Mr Pyke, who had been standing in the background looking sheepish, gathered the remains of his dignity and stalked forward.

'Hah! Of course, Prince!' he rasped. 'I – er – regret jumping on you as I did, but – er – anyone might have made the same mistake.'

'You think so?' returned Mr Prince coldly. 'At least, I'm glad Mr Quinn here made no mistake.'

'Hah!' Pyke snorted. 'It was the sheerest luck he had that contraption in his pocket.'

'I think there was judgement as well as luck, sir,' put in Lady Barry. 'Neither of them your strong point, alas!'

The look that Lieutenant Pyke threw at Septimus was, as the midshipman afterwards remarked, a scorcher.

'Come!' said the Bow Street man, producing a stout rope from the boot. 'Get my man safely tied, and on we go to Portsmouth.'

'Mr Quinn!' growled Lieutenant Pyke between his teeth. 'Be so good as to lend a hand here.'

Septimus raised his cocked hat.

'Aye, aye, sir!' he said.

4

The London Mail drew up outside the George in Portsmouth half-an-hour behind time, and a crowd gathered from nowhere to watch the captured and scowling Jeremy Craw taken off to the local gaol. Septimus Quinn had to receive the thanks of Lady Barry and Philippa, and give his name and address to Mr Prince (who assured him that fifty guineas would shortly be placed to his credit in the bank) before he could get away.

It was a relief to escape from the neighbourhood of Lieutenant Pyke, whose wounded pride kept him in a state of ill-temper that would not have disgraced an active volcano. Septimus felt sorry for Philippa's brother Charles, who had to be in the same ship with such a curmudgeon. Possibly, he reflected, his career in the Navy might at some time bring him into contact with Lieutenant Pyke again, but he hoped it would not be for very many years.

He got a man with a barrow to take his sea-chest down to the docks. The evening was clearing into sunshine as he stood on the quayside, where a thousand gulls wheeled and screamed above the masts and rigging of a multitude of ships of all kinds. A waterman in a broad-beamed wherry sculled his craft alongside and looked up at him.

'What ship are ye for, sir? Frigate *Althea*? Layin' to moorings over yonder – put ye aboard in five minutes.'

Septimus handed down his sea-chest and got into the wherry. As it shoved off and headed out into the crowded harbour he wondered how long it would be before he set foot on shore again, and what adventures would have befallen him before he came back.

The waterman eyed him knowingly. 'Fust ship ye've jined, sir?' he asked. 'She's a good 'un, the *Althea*. Cap'n Sainsbury, he's a proper fire-eater. But they do say as the Fust Lootenant's a rare narsty bit o' work.'

This last news was not encouraging. But Septimus cheered himself with the thought that the First Lieutenant of the *Althea* could hardly be as nasty as Lieutenant Pyke.

'Yonder's your vssel, sir,' said the waterman, jerking his head. 'His Majesty's frigate *Althea*.'

Septimus craned his neck to stare ahead. A tall ship, lean of hull, with a long bowsprit thrusting forward like a fencer's foil, lay motionless on the calm harbour waters. The black-painted oaken side of her was lined with a broad band of white, in which gaped the row of open gun-ports. Her three slender masts towered overhead into the golden sunshine, reaching up and up until it seemed a wonder that the *Althea* didn't overturn with such gigantic structures rearing from her decks. As the wherry came closer Septimus could see tiny figures perched high up in the web-like rigging; sometimes they swung from place to place like spiders on a thread. The clear note of a bell floated across the water: *dong-dong, dong-dong.*

'Four bells,' said the waterman. 'Ship's time, that is – ye'll be livin' by that soon. I'll pull round to the larboard side,' he added.

As the wherry came close under the frigate's side – it looked an enormous wooden wall from that angle – a voice hailed the boat loudly: 'Boat ahoy!'

'Aye aye!' roared the waterman in reply. ' 'Ear what I said?' he added to Septimus. ' "Aye aye" means there's an officer in my boat. If there 'adn't been, I'd 'ave said "no-no", see?'

It was dawning on Septimus that in stepping aboard the *Althea*, his new home, he was entering a world entirely different from anything he had known, with a new language, new ways of telling the time, and the new and somewhat awesome surroundings. To get into it, apparently, he had to climb up a dangling ladder made of slats of wood and lengths of rope. Being agile and neat in his movements, he managed it without trouble and arrived on deck. A thin, youngish officer, with a telescope tucked under his arm, had been awaiting him. Septimus had not yet learned that everyone salutes the quarterdeck as they step on board a warship – a custom dating from the days when a Crucifix always stood there – but he remembered to lift his hat to the officer.

'Septimus Quinn, midshipman – sir,' he said as confidently as he could.

'Come aboard, Mr Quinn.' The officer had a pleasant smile. 'I'm Lieutenant Gifford. Sea-chest? I'll have it sent to the gun-room where your berth is.'

It was at this moment that a tall, red-faced man strode across the deck some yards away and disappeared down a hatchway. Septimus stared after him.

'P-pray, sir, who was that?' he stammered.

'That was the First Lieutenant of this vessel,' replied Lieutenant Gifford. 'His name is Pyke, Lieutenant George Pyke.'

Chapter Two

Masthead

I

His Majesty's frigate *Althea* was pounding southward through the heavy seas of the Bay of Biscay. A westerly gale had blown for two days and she was carrying very little canvas on the three tall masts that leaned over before the wind, their taut rigging making wild shrill music. A hundred and thirty feet above the wet slant of the deck the lookout crouched in the crow's-nest, occasionally bobbing up to peer round the stormy horizon of sea. With Nelson on watch in the Mediterranean there was little likelihood of any French warship being sighted in these waters, and all the lookout could have reported was that the gale was getting worse. He looked up frequently at the foretopmast above his head, where Mr Pyke, the *Althea*'s First Lieutenant, had seen fit to have a reefed topsail set.

'That rag ole Lobsterface 'as 'ung out won't stand much more o' this,' muttered the lookout at intervals. Lobsterface was the nickname the *Althea*'s crew used for her First Lieutenant – never, of course, to that violent-tempered officer's face.

Down below decks, in the smelly, candle-lit section of the gunroom where the midshipmen had their quarters, three young gentlemen were discussing navigation. Or rather, the largest and oldest of the three was giving his opinion on the navigation which they had been taught during the ten days they had been at sea. Fitzroy Cocker was eighteen, tall and redhaired, and had a temper that matched his hair.

'It's a lot of mumbo-jumbo, demme!' he declared. 'All this rigmarole about angles and sextants – it don't make sense. If an officer's got a shipmaster to lay him alongside a Frenchman, that's all he wants, and it's good enough for me, demme!'

As he spoke he was balancing himself between the wooden bulkhead and the fixed table, for the whole of the cabin was tilted at a steep angle. He also had to speak at the top of his loud voice because of the continuous noise of creaking, grinding, banging and howling made by the ship as she fought her way through the storm.

Midshipman the Hon. Charles Barry, a slim dark boy two years younger than Cocker, looked up from the tattered book he was trying to study by the flickering light of the candle.

'Well, we've got to learn the stuff, Fitz,' he said. 'Might as well buckle to and get it over.'

'Bah!' spat Cocker impatiently. He swung round to scowl at the third midshipman, an undersized youngster who was peering through steel-rimmed spectacles at some pencilled calculations he had been making. 'As for you, young lickspittle, I suppose you're pretending to like it – currying favour with the senior officers, eh?'

'Pray sir,' retorted Septimus Quinn mildly, 'do you really think I've curried any favour with our dear First Lieutenant?'

Charles Barry laughed. 'That's true enough, Fitz. Mr Pyke's done nothing but curse our spectacled midshipman and try to catch him out ever since Quinn joined.'

This was not strictly true, but there was truth in it. The First Lieutenant of the frigate had had a great many more important things to do than look for chances of venting his wrath on a junior midshipman; but Mr George Pyke had made a point of being thoroughly unpleasant whenever Septimus Quinn crossed his path. Septimus had not breathed a word about the encounter with the highwayman on the journey to Portsmouth, but the seamen had picked up some of the tale in the Portsmouth taverns and it was whispered about the ship that young Mr Quinn had foiled a desperate toby-man while 'old Lobsterface' sat still and shouted for help – which was rather unfair to Mr Pyke.

Septimus had taken a week to get used to the new life of serving in a King's ship, and then had settled into it with the ease of a philosopher. He had quickly learned that he was now the humblest unit in a floating community of two hundred men, where Duty was the most important thing. According to Captain Sainsbury, the ruler of this tiny wooden-walled community, Duty meant knowing exactly what an order meant and obeying that order quickly and correctly even though it meant death to do so. Septimus could see that this was a vital necessity in a ship of war, but he reflected that part of his own duty would be to give orders – when he had learned his job – and that meant that he would be using his own initiative instead of blindly obeying the orders of Lieutenant Pyke or Lieutenant Gifford. It was the thought of some day being able to command and plan for himself that encouraged young Mr Quinn to stick at his studies of Navigation and Seamanship, much to the disgust of the fault-finding Lieutenant Pyke.

After one first interview, Septimus had seen little of Captain Sainsbury, a dark and silent man who very seldom smiled. Mr Pyke was supposed to oversee the instruction of the three midshipmen, and though they were taught navigation by Mr Haswell, the elderly Third Lieutenant, and seamanship by Preece the gunner's mate, the red face of the First Lieutenant was always thrusting itself unexpectedly into their lessons and barking difficult questions at them. He fired his hardest questions at Septimus, but so far the junior midshipman had not given one wrong answer – which seemed only to increase Mr Pyke's dislike of him. Pyke was always particularly nice to Charles Barry, though Barry was far from bright at navigation, and he had little to say to Fitzroy Cocker, who was as tall as himself and related to an important Member of Parliament. It was Septimus Quinn's blood he was after. Cocker was accustomed to say that if Lobsterface didn't catch out young lick-spittle soon he'd burst.

Septimus naturally saw a great deal of the other two midshipmen, and had sized them up in his own quiet fashion. Charles Barry was handsome, inclined to be lazy, and had far less spirit (so

The *Althea* Frigate at Moorings, Gibraltar.
A Drawing in Midshipman Quinn's private Log.

Septimus thought) than his pretty sister Philippa who had shown fight when the highwaymen stopped the coach. Fitzroy Cocker might be as eager to fight the French as he boasted, but Septimus had formed a poor opinion of his brain. The red-haired senior midshipman never thought before he acted and did not conceal his contempt for the small quiet boy who had joined the *Althea* without knowing a bowsprit from a mainyard. Cocker had been in the frigate for nearly a year and had sailed to Majorca and back, and having in that time learned to swear and gamble, considered himself a very experienced sea-officer indeed. However, Septimus was not the boy to look at the worst side of his companions for long. He could admire Cocker's strength and keenness for a fight, and he liked Barry's lazy good manners, though neither of them had shown much liking for him. Mr Septimus Quinn was never much concerned as to whether folk liked him or not.

As he was applying himself once again to the problem of a vessel's course from Ushant to the Balearic Isles, an unusually violent gust heeled the frigate still further over for a few seconds. Charles Barry clutched at the table and looked rather apprehensively at his messmates.

'She's – she's lying over a bit, isn't she?' he remarked, trying to sound calm.

Cocker laughed scornfully. 'Bah! This is nothing. Wait till you're in a real South Atlantic snorter, my boy. You'll have to sleep on the bulkhead and use the deck to hang your hat on – that's the sort of angle she'll take then!'

'All the same,' observed Septimus, looking up over the rims of his spectacles, 'this isn't the South Atlantic. If I were Mr Pyke, who is in charge of the deck just now, I would take in that reefed fore-topsail. That was what—'

'Oh, you would?' sneered Cocker, turning on him. 'And who asked you to speak? "In charge of the deck," demme! I suppose you mean Pyke has the watch-on-deck. What the Hades do you know about topsails, hey?'

'I was about to say,' ventured Septimus mildly, 'that Mr Preece made that observation a short while ago. I was merely repeating—'

'Well, keep your baby mouth shut!' interrupted the senior midshipman curtly. 'Preece is a gunner's mate, not a First Lieutenant. There, she's righted herself. First-rate little warship, *Althea* is, mark my words.'

Mr Quinn blinked owlishly at him through his spectacles.

'It is reassuring to know that she compares so favourably with all the other ships you have sailed in,' he said innocently.

Cocker, red in the face, started to gobble a reply and then, finding it difficult to make a proper retort, turned to Barry.

'I'm sick of sitting here like a demmed schoolboy,' he snapped. 'What's the hour, Charles?'

'Six bells went a few minutes ago – didn't you hear them? We're supposed to go on studying for another half-hour, you know. That's why we're let off deck watch.'

'Let off!' Cocker repeated, mimicking Barry's tone. 'Why, no officer of spirit would want to be "let off" a watch-on-deck. I'd ten times rather be standing a trick at the wheel than cooped up down here with you two swots. It's no occupation for a gentleman, demme! So – belay it, Charles.' He leaned forward and twitched Barry's book away from him, to send it spinning into a corner. We'll spend the rest of our watch-below to better advantage, hey?'

Barry looked annoyed at this high-handed action, but only for a moment.

'Oh, all right, then,' he responded half-heartedly, holding on to the table as the *Althea* gave another lurch. 'What's it to be, Fitz?'

'What but the gentleman's game, my boy – dice!' Cocker produced a small ebony dice-box from his coat pocket and slapped it on the table, holding it on the tilted and swaying surface with his palm. 'A main with you messmates!'

'The dice will fly all over the cabin,' protested Charles. 'And besides—'

'Besides, we're supposed to go on studying,' Cocker mimicked him again. 'Demme, forget your studies in a little sport, man! We'll shake 'em in the box, set the box on the table, and that's the throw. And you, young lickspittle,' he added to Septimus, 'you're in this too, so set aside that paper and be sociable.'

'My name, Mr Cocker, is Quinn, if you please,' said Septimus gently. 'And I am not interested in dice.'

Charles Barry patted him on the shoulder. 'Oh, come on, Quinn,' he said with his engaging smile. 'Fitz can't help being rude. I can't see to read by this candle, anyhow.'

Septimus hesitated. Games of chance struck him as being unscientific and therefore uninteresting, and though he had an ample money allowance to supplement his pay he had no mind to risk it on the throw of a pair of dice. All the same, he didn't want to put on the airs of a self-righteous prig. For months, perhaps years, he would be living at very close quarters with these two, and already his application to his studies had made an enemy of the arrogant Fitzroy Cocker. It was all very well to be self-sufficient at Linton Abbott, where he could escape to the woods and fields of the countryside when he felt inclined for solitude, but here things were very different. There was no room for an independent spirit in a small fighting-ship where every man was dependent on his shipmates and the Captain alone had any privacy. So Septimus decided it was time he showed a comradely spirit.

'Very well,' he agreed, slipping paper and pencil into his pocket. 'Pray allow me to join you. How are we to play?'

'It had better be made easy for our mathematical genius,' sneered Cocker, rattling the dice. 'Stake what you like, winner take all. No limits. Money on the table – it won't slide off, quite. Here's mine.'

He slammed a golden half-guinea on the table with a glance at Septimus.

'Here, I say, Fitz!' Barry protested. 'We're midshipmen, not Nabobs worth fifty thousand apiece!'

'It's my custom to play high on the first throw,' explained Cocker loftily. 'No need for you youngsters to imitate me. Stake up, now!'

Barry fished in his pockets and put a silver crown-piece on the table. Septimus laid a sixpence carefully in front of him, and looked inquiringly at Cocker. That young gentleman's lip curled, but he refrained from comment.

'We'll throw in alphabetical order,' he announced. 'You first, then me, then Quinn. Here you are.'

He tossed the dice-box to Barry, who put his palm over the open top and shook the dice heartily before setting the box down on the slanting table-top. Cocker leaned across to peer at the little ivory cubes as they came to rest.

'Nine!' he shouted. 'A stout try, Charles – but there's room for me.'

He shook the box and thumped it down.

'Pipped me by one,' Barry said cheerfully, passing the dice-box to Septimus. 'You'll need luck to beat ten, Quinn.'

Septimus nodded. He was not interested in luck. He gave the box a quick twirl and set it down. Cocker and Barry craned their heads to look into it, and Cocker swore loudly.

'There's the devil's own luck for you!' he growled. 'Double six! Well, pay up and stake again.'

He and Barry pushed their stakes towards the winner, and Septimus, displaying no satisfaction at winning fifteen shillings and sixpence, was just gathering up the coins when the wrathful red face of the First Lieutenant appeared without warning from the shadows.

The three midshipmen all scrambled to their feet (Cocker, in spite of his boasted sea experience, banging his head on the low deck-beams) and stood as stiffly as the lurching of the ship would allow.

'Hah!' barked Mr Pyke with satisfaction. 'Caught red-handed, I think. Until eight bells of the afternoon watch you were to study. How, may I ask, does it come about that I find you gaming?'

'Because the ship-noises prevented us from hearing you coming, sir,' answered Cocker brazenly.

From anyone else such impertinence would have met with the First Lieutenant's heavy-handed retribution. As it was Fitzroy Cocker, Pyke merely snorted.

'Hah! And whose idea was this piece of disobedience?' he demanded.

No one answered this time. Pyke's bulging blue eyes turned to Septimus Quinn, whose fingers were still on the coins.

'There's no need to tell me,' he barked accusingly. 'Mr Midshipman Quinn has been winning, I see. I'll wager a guinea he knows how to turn the dice, and I'll wager another one that he started the game. Pipe down, you, sir!' he added fiercely as Charles Barry tried to protest. 'I shall ask Mr Quinn some questions and we will see if he can answer them. Now, Mr Quinn!'

'Now, sir,' said Septimus politely.

Pyke's red face went a shade redder.

'Attend to me!' he rasped. 'And answer correctly or it'll be the worse for you. A vessel in latitude 44 degrees and 30 minutes north, longitude 9 degrees 36 minutes west – course south by west – *where is she and where's she heading*? Quick, now!'

Now it so happened that Septimus had taken the trouble to find out certain facts from Mr Preece the gunner's mate, and these facts were the very ones mentioned by Pyke. He answered like lightning.

'Position, forty miles nor'west of Cape Ortegal, sir. Heading to round Cape Finisterre on the Galician coast.'

'Hah!' The First Lieutenant tried to conceal his disappointment by barking another question. 'Then what else d'ye know about this vessel?'

'She is the frigate *Althea*,' replied the midshipman. 'Thirty-eight guns, Captain Sainsbury.' And now it was that he made the mistake of being too clever. 'Carrying a reefed topsail on the fore,' he added deliberately, 'which, in this gale, is bad seamanship.'

Fitzroy Cocker said afterwards that he thought Lieutenant Pyke would have an apoplexy. Certainly that officer's face went a deep purple, and for a second or two he was unable to speak.

'You – you confounded impertinent pup!' he burst out at last. 'I'll – by heaven, I'll teach you! Bad seamanship! What do *you* know about it?' He stopped suddenly and his glaring eyes narrowed. 'I'll send you somewhere where you can learn a little more seamanship, Mr Septimus Quinn. To the main-mast-head!'

2

It was not an uncommon punishment for midshipmen to be 'mastheaded' – sent to the top of the ship's mainmast to stay there until they were told to come down. But to send a boy there in a full gale, with the ship lying over on her side and the masts swooping and rearing before the gusts, was an almost unheard-of thing. Both the older midshipmen looked shocked, and Cocker even began a stammering protest which a glare from the First Lieutenant instantly silenced. As for Septimus, he took off his spectacles and put them into their case, trying hard not to show his dismay.

'That was an order, sir!' roared Mr Pyke. 'Up to the masthead with you, and step lively or I'll have you in irons!'

'Aye aye, sir!' said Septimus smartly, and made for the companionway leading to the deck.

As he passed Barry, he felt something pushed urgently against him, and grasped it. It was Barry's tarpaulin coat.

Lieutenant Pyke followed him on deck without another word, and turned his back on Septimus to go to the quarterdeck. The midshipman wriggled into the waterproof jacket before crossing the slippery deck. To gain the weather bulwarks he had to claw his way up a slope of wet planking against repeated showers of spray, and when he climbed into the mainmast rigging – where horizontal rope 'ratlines' between the straining stays of the mast made a precarious ladder – a positive spout of sea water lashed him from head to foot and would have soaked him to the skin had it not been for Barry's tarpaulin coat. Flattened against the rigging by the wind, he began to climb.

With the frigate heeled over at so steep an angle, the first part of the climb was not particularly difficult. The mainmast was leaning away from him, so that the ascent of the shrouds was not so steep as it would have been if she had been on an even keel. But the fury of the gale, and its hundreds of deafening voices, was bewildering. The great mainyard was braced round, and although the mainsail was double-reefed its big curve of canvas was trembling and thundering as if it would tear itself away at any moment. Every rope in the network of cordage that supported the *Althea*'s three masts sang shrilly with its own particular note, and the din of the seas against her wooden hull added a deeper note to the chorus.

Septimus did not hesitate, in such weather, to use the 'lubber's hole' when he came to the maintop, the wooden platform from the edges of which ran the shrouds supporting the upper part of the mast. The frigate's topmen, the chosen seamen who could go aloft in all weathers to reef or furl sails, disdained this easy way cut in the platform, and would always climb over its edge by means of the futtock-shrouds, hanging on with their backs turned to the deck far below. But Septimus was not a topman. As Mr Pyke very well knew, this monkey-like climbing in the spider's-web of the rigging was the one thing Septimus most disliked.

On the reeling planking of the maintop he paused for breath, with his arms hugging the big mast itself. The mast was groaning like a monster in pain, and he could feel its vibration under the force of the wind. But he felt certain that Lieutenant Pyke was watching him, and his pride would not let him pause too long. Setting his teeth, he swung himself round on to the shrouds again and fought his way upward.

The long ladder of rope was not at all steady. It slackened a little as the *Althea* rolled, then tautened suddenly again with a horrible creaking noise. Septimus was jerked and swung as he clutched and grabbed and clutched again, and he was exceedingly frightened, though he refused to admit it in his mind. Up, and up, and up, with the wild swerving of the mast growing ever more violent. It seemed a very long time before he got his weary hands over the topsail yard and somehow hauled himself on to it, to sit with his short legs dangling over the long spar and his arms clasped tightly round the topmast.

For a moment he stayed like that, with his eyes shut. The mast was like a bucking horse under him, trying to throw him off.

Remembering that the three midshipmen had been wearing tarpaulin coats when last Mr Preece instructed them in rope-splicing, he contrived to feel in the pocket of Barry's coat. As he expected, the fathom of light line used for splicing practice was coiled up in the pocket. Perched as he was, it was a perilous business getting the rope out and uncoiled, and when he did succeed in freeing it the wind streamed it out horizontally and all but snatched it from his hand. With infinite care he pushed one end of the line through the stout leather belt he wore and managed to lead it round the mast. A moment later he had joined the ends with a reef knot and was lashed securely to the mast.

Now, at last, he could look about him in safety – though not in comfort. His first glance showed him hurrying dark clouds overhead, clouds that seemed to race and halt and spin in every direction. When he realised that it was he, and not the clouds, that swung so violently between sea and sky, he felt sick and dizzy and had to shut his eyes again for a while. When he opened them it was to look down, and that downward glance was a terrifying one.

Directly beneath him, very far below, was the angry sea, grey-green waves racing away from the ship's lee side and showing their white teeth in ridges of foam. Bringing his gaze inward a little he saw the frigate's deck looking like the deck of a toy ship, so small it seemed from that height above. At first he could see no human figures, for the men at the helm were hidden by the rigging and reefed sails of the mizzen-mast. But soon he made out a little group of men huddled under the weather bulwarks – the watch-on-deck standing by to obey any orders from the quarterdeck – and the sight made him feel a little less lonely up there on his reeling masthead.

Septimus was getting used to the dizzy circling of his wooden perch now, but it had needed considerable resolution to prevent himself from being sick. It was his habit, when in uncomfortable or dangerous situations, to look for the brighter aspects of such situations; and to take his mind off the ceaseless jerking and swaying he set himself to do so now. The outlook from the mainmast-head had nothing bright about it. On every side was the notchy black horizon of a stormy sea raging beneath a stormy sky. But Mr Pyke's vindictive punishment had shown up two bright spots – the sympathy of his brother midshipmen. Cocker had made an attempt to protest against that punishment, Barry had made him take the tarpaulin jacket which was protecting him now – a welcome protection, for though it was August the gale had a bite in it. Septimus knew that his two messmates had a poor opinion of him, and he had held no very high opinion of them. This was the first time they had shown that they counted him as their comrade, for they had undoubtedly been on his side and against Pyke's revengeful order. He reflected that Cocker could not, after all, be quite such a bully as he tried to appear, and that Charles Barry had shown unexpected forethought in thrusting the jacket into his hand.

Another thought crossed his mind, too. It was easy enough to score off the quick-tempered First Lieutenant, but it would have been much wiser to hold his tongue when he knew that Mr Pyke could inflict so uncomfortable a punishment. Mr Midshipman Quinn was discovering that he had much to learn about men, as well as about ships.

His cheek was pressed against the smooth cold wood of the topmast, and it hid the forepart of the ship from him. Peering round it now, he could see the *Althea*'s foremast little more than fifty feet away from him in mid-air. The highest tip of the foretopmast was just level with him. Below it, bellying from the yard and looking as if it was about to fly off across the ocean, was the reefed topsail which Lieutenant Pyke had ordered to be set and which Septimus had been unwise enough to criticise. Looking at its straining curve, he remembered what Mr Preece had so confidentially told him that afternoon.

'Them topmast stays do need new-rigging, indeed,' the Welsh gunner's mate had said. 'I tell you now, Mr Quinn, sir, that it is tamn foolishness to hoist a tops'l – reef or no reef – on that mast in such a blow. Yess, indeed. But there is no telling Mr Pyke. No, indeed!'

It would be a nasty mess, thought Septimus, if the rigging

parted and the topmast came crashing down, as it would do. Its many stays would keep it from hurtling to the deck, but the seamen would have a difficult and dangerous job to clear the tangle in this gale. Lowering his gaze a little, he saw the round barrel-shape of the crow's-nest at the foot of the topmast, and the head and shoulders of the lookout protruding from it. Since there was little danger of hostile warships appearing in the Bay of Biscay, the lookout's main duty was to scan the seas ahead for possible floating wreckage or other obstructions dangerous to a speeding vessel, and the man had apparently not seen the midshipman behind and above him. Septimus thought he recognised that mop of tow-coloured hair and those broad shoulders. It was a man called Tod Beamish, a seaman of gigantic size and immense strength.

An extra strong gust sent the frigate heeling over another five degrees and Septimus tightened his clutch on the mast. For a few sickening seconds he had the impression that she was going to turn completely over. Then she recovered herself, the tall mast to which he clung rising slowly again to its former angle. Of course the *Althea* was built to withstand such tremendous thrusts – he told himself that and felt reassured. All the same, the strain on that topmast with its violently-tugging sail must have been very great. He thanked his lucky stars that Lieutenant Pyke had not seen fit to hoist a reefed topsail on his own mast.

Already it seemed a long time since he had arrived at his present airy perch. How long, he wondered, would Pyke leave him up there? Presumably until Captain Sainsbury was due to come on deck. Septimus felt reasonably certain that the *Althea*'s captain would order him down as soon as he discovered what Pyke had done. Among the frigate's crew it was said that Sainsbury was a hard man but just. He was not the officer to send a midshipman to the masthead in a full gale.

Septimus began to feel chilled and weak. He tried to forget his discomforts in thinking of the blue Mediterranean waters which they would be entering in a few days. What the *Althea* was to do in the Mediterranean he did not know. Captain Sainsbury was the only man aboard the frigate who knew what orders had been given him by Their Lordships of the Admiralty, and if he chose to keep those orders secret he could do so. The all-knowing Mr Preece, placing a horny finger alongside his bulbous nose and looking extremely wise, had given it as his opinion that they were sailing under sealed orders.

'Cap'n, he'll open them orders when we reaches Gibraltar,' he had said. 'And if, as I thinks, we'm bound for an independent cruise – why, now, young gents, there'll be fighting a-plenty and prize-money for every man Jack. Yess, indeed!'

The promise of fighting did not greatly excite Septimus. It was not pleasing to him to contemplate a hand-to-hand struggle with a Frenchman. But he knew that before and during and after such struggles a delicate science was brought into play, a science of manœuvring for position, changing direction of attack, drawing off one's forces in a prudent and subtle manner. It was this side of warfare that appealed to young Mr Quinn. In imagining himself in command of a cutter detailed to surprise a French garrison by night, he almost forgot the increasing discomfort of his position.

He was just at the point in his imaginary expedition when, having made a feint attack on the front of the enemy position, he led a desperate assault on the flank, when his vaguely-roaming eye saw the thin black line across the sky to windward. It was a long line of cloud, rapidly approaching, and he knew that it was what seamen called 'a line squall'. When that ominous line reached the *Althea* she would feel the sudden smiting of the squall – only for a moment, but the blow would be a heavy one. Septimus wondered whether those on deck had seen the coming danger, and clutched his topmast more tightly. Faint shouts from below told him that Mr Pyke had seen the squall. The tiny figures of men ran across the deck in readiness to brace the yards, for the helmsman would bring the frigate's bows into the wind a little to meet the squall.

The line of cloud was almost upon them now. He felt the sudden increase of wind-pressure and the bending of the mast before it. The frigate dipped and swerved and Septimus swung like an inverted pendulum out and downward over the frothing sea. He closed his eyes – and then opened them quickly, for a splintering *cr-r-ack*! had come to his ears above the din of sea and wind.

He was in time to see the top spar of the foremast, only a short distance in front of him, lean over towards him faster and faster until it crashed down to hang with its rag of topsail torn and fluttering.

3

Septimus did not at first realise the significance of the frightened shout which the wind carried to his ears. Then he remembered the lookout, and peered anxiously to see what had happened to him.

The fore-topmast had broken off at its base, just where the barrel-like crow's-nest was secured. It had snapped off cleanly, falling backwards and downward until the network of rigging had arrested it, and its tip had caught in the fore rigging of the mainmast almost directly beneath the place where Septimus was perched. The crow's-nest had been knocked into matchwood by the snapping mast and there was no sign of the man who had been in it.

As Septimus craned his neck to look downwards he felt the frigate righting herself after the squall, and heard the distant voices, like seagull-cries, of men on the deck very far below him. And then he saw the lookout.

The man was clinging to the broken butt of the topmast, swinging in mid-air nearly a hundred feet above the deck. It was Tod Beamish, right enough – and he appeared to be hurt. He was astride the hanging mast, with arms and legs clasped round it, and was slowly and painfully hitching himself along it towards the end that rested in the mainmast rigging. But he was moving very slowly, and Septimus could see the blood running from a big cut on his head. With every lurch of the ship the dangling butt of the mast swung back and forth. The fallen mast was not quite horizontal, he noted – the butt was lower than the tip, so that Beamish was edging upward. Thirty feet below him the midshipman could see the end of the mast resting on the shrouds. It was only just reaching them. An extra violent roll would dislodge it, and Beamish would be hurled to the deck and killed outright.

So far as he could see, those on deck had not seen the lookout's plight. Men were running towards the base of the foremast, some carrying axes, and it was plain that they would climb to the foretop and try to clear the tangle. From the foretop they could do nothing to help Beamish. He raised his voice in a desperate shout.

'Deck, there! Deck!'

But the gale carried his words away. Probably no one knew of his presence at the masthead except Lieutenant Pyke, and Pyke would have forgotten him in the urgency of the need for clearing the dangling topmast. Septimus felt very much alone. He thought of descending to the deck – but he was no topman and the descent would take him several minutes. He peered again at Beamish.

The man had heard his shout. He had wormed his way along the spar until he was almost at its end where it was lodged in the rigging, but there he had stopped. His big face, white with pain and fear, was looking up at Septimus appealingly. The *Althea* rolled slightly, and the sway of the spar nearly dislodged him. Plainly he was near to losing consciousness and dared not try to move further.

Septimus Quinn woke suddenly to the realisation that if Tod Beamish's life was to be saved he would have to act, and act quickly.

'Beamish!' he shouted with the full force of his lungs. 'Hold on, man – I'm coming to you!'

As he shouted he was untying the knot that secured him to the main topmast, thanking his stars that he had tied a reef and not a 'granny', which would have jammed. The furious blast of the gale, the dizzy swooping of the mast, were forgotten now that there was something vitally urgent to be done. He gripped the loosened line between his teeth and took one glance at the way he had to go.

The thrumming shrouds seemed to fall away into grey space

from his feet. Resting on them, thirty feet down, was the tip of the mast. He could see it shifting very slightly as the frigate lurched, and every movement was edging it further from its resting-place. A two-inch shift, and it would come adrift and fall until it hung straight down. He had not a second to spare.

Down the shrouds he went, as fast as he dared with that wind tearing at him. He reached the place where the mast had come to rest. It had broken two of the ratlines in its fall, he saw. Beamish was only seven or eight feet away, lying along the mast with arms and legs locked round it. His eyes were closed and his face was white as paper. Septimus did his best to speak cheerfully, though he could see that he had taken on an extremely difficult and perilous task.

'All right, Beamish – you're all right. I'm here to give you a hand. But you must make an effort. Come along, now!'

Beamish opened his eyes, but closed them again at once. His only answer was a groan. Septimus tried again.

'It's only about a fathom you've to go, man. Summon all your strength. Look – here's my hand stretched out ready for you. When you can grasp it you're safe.'

'I – I can't,' gasped the man. 'I'm done, Mr Quinn, sir. If I move I'll fall – I know I'll fall.'

Septimus glanced down at the round spar whose end lay on the frail rung of rope between his feet. It had moved another fraction of an inch, outward, away from the shrouds. The frigate was maintaining a fairly steady heel, but even if she made no specially violent lurch the continual rocking of her masts must very soon dislodge the spar. His glance, passing the spar, went through empty air to the deck directly beneath him. The tiny figures of seamen were clustered down there, pointing upward and gesticulating. The drama being enacted in mid-air had been seen. Help would come now, but it would take time, and there were only seconds to spare. Septimus made his plan and acted on it at once.

His only apparatus was the six feet of line which had secured him to the mast. He turned round on the ladder-like shrouds so that he was standing face outwards with his heels lodged precariously on the horizontal ropes and the end of the spar between his knees. He had to use both hands to make his next move, and it was not easy. Passing one end of the line round the spar, he secured it loosely with a bowline loop so that the loop would slide along the spar. Then, with the other end held between his teeth, he crouched and carefully bent forward until both hands were gripping the round wood. A second later he was lying along the spar with his head towards Beamish.

The spar sloped slightly downwards. He wondered, as he made the move, whether his extra weight would slide it from its place. He was surprised to find that he was not afraid – the question of whether he and Beamish would be hurtling down to death in the next half-second seemed no more important than a problem in navigation. He began to edge himself along towards Beamish.

Only a few feet separated them, but he had to get close up to Beamish's body before he could carry out his plan. As he wriggled along with arms locked round the topmast, he slid the loop of line before him. Now he was within an inch or two of Beamish's head. The seaman was motionless with his cheek pressed tightly against the spar and his eyes closed.

'Keep holding on,' he said reassuringly, speaking with difficulty because of the line in his teeth. 'Five seconds, and you'll be perfectly safe.'

Beamish made no sign. The midshipman moved forward until his raised head was beyond that of the helpless man, and then, gripping with his knees and one hand, took the end of the line in the other. Like all seamen, Beamish wore a stout leather belt. To get the end of the line under that belt while barely keeping himself from being blown or flung off the swaying spar was the worst task Septimus had ever had to perform. It seemed an age before he succeeded in getting the line threaded and the end pulled back. Then he had to knot it – with one hand. And the knot must be absolutely secure. It was Mr Preece who had taught him to tie a bowline one-handed, and now that bit of practical knowledge was worth a man's life.

At last it was done. The length of line had one end secured to the spar and the other to Beamish's belt. The man was safe for the moment – so long as the spar kept in its place.

'Listen, Beamish.' Septimus spoke with his mouth close to the man's ear. 'You're lashed to this spar. If you slip, you won't fall. So you can safely finish the trip. Do you understand?'

'I unnerstand,' Beamish said faintly. 'But I've got no strength left. I can't move – I can't, sir!'

'You can,' said the midshipman firmly. 'And you're going to. I'm going to tow you – and you'll have to help me or I'll fall off myself. Come on – *heave*!'

As he spoke the word, he got his free hand into the seaman's collar and began to edge back again towards the shrouds.

Wriggling backwards and slightly uphill, he could really exert very little force on Beamish, who was twice his size. But the slight pull, and his cheerful 'Heave ho! Heave!' brought to the half-conscious seaman enough encouragement to make him use his failing strength in one last effort. Inch by inch the two hitched themselves towards safety. Septimus felt the shrouds behind him and reached for a grip on them. Beamish was almost within reach of them. He looked at the end of the spar. It was very near falling – and Beamish was tied to it.

'Steady does it,' said Septimus between his teeth. And, as Beamish reached both hands and grasped the shrouds, he plucked the man's sheath-knife from his waist and slashed through the linking line.

He had barely done so, and got his hand once more to Beamish's collar to haul him the last foot, when the spar slipped from the cordage and swung down into space.

'*Hang on*!' yelled the midshipman.

But Beamish was safely planted, with both feet in the shrouds and his big hands locked on the rope.

Septimus, keeping one hand pressed against the seaman's broad back, prayed that he would not lose consciousness now. He himself was feeling very shaky after that effort and could do little more than keep himself from falling. But voices, breathless and anxious, hailed him from close below.

'Hold on, sir! . . . We're coming!'

Half-a-dozen topmen were racing up the mainmast shrouds to their assistance. In less that a minute brawny arms were grasping them. With an agile seaman on each side of them, the rescuer and the rescued were brought down to the deck and safety.

4

'I'm no hand at speeches, Mr Quinn, sir,' said Tod Beamish, looking down awkwardly from his six-and-a-half feet, 'but – well, I'd not be here, but for you. Thankee, sir.'

'Pray don't mention it, Beamish,' replied Mr Midshipman Quinn gravely. 'Who knows? You may have occasion to do the same for me one day.'

It was the morning after Septimus had been sent to the mast-head, and the *Althea* was flying across a rolling blue sea under all plain sail. The gale had blown itself out in the night. From the maindeck where the two were standing, swaying easily to the motion of the vessel, the Spanish coast could just be seen as a long pale-brown line on the eastern horizon.

'I trust,' Septimus added, 'that your head is mending?'

Beamish raised a hand to the bandage that swathed his tow-coloured head.

'Mending well, sir,' he grinned. 'Surgeon says it's lucky it was me head that was hit – any other part of me would have been bust good and proper, he says.'

He knuckled his forehead in a gesture of salute and trotted away, as Midshipman the Honourable Charles Barry, very trim in his uniform coat with telescope under arm, hurried up from the direction of the quarterdeck.

'Captain's compliments, Mr Quinn,' he said with great solemnity, 'and he'll be infinitely obliged if you'd do him the honour of being so good to step on to the quarterdeck for a word with him.'

'Pray inform Captain Sainsbury that I can spare him a moment of my valuable time and will be with him directly,' returned Septimus with equal solemnity.

'And you'd better step lively, Sep,' added Barry, a grin displacing his gravity. 'You know he don't like to be kept waiting.'

As he made all speed for the quarterdeck, Septimus remembered Charles Barry's silent grip of the hand when he had come down from his ordeal of yesterday, and felt that he was no longer 'one out' in the midshipmen's berth.

Captain Sainsbury, a tall lean figure in blue coat and white knee-breeches, was standing at the quarterdeck rail gazing towards the coast of Spain. He raised a thin hand to his cocked hat in acknowledgement of the midshipman's stiff salute, and then turned away to resume his gazing.

'Mr Quinn,' he said without looking round, 'I do not propose to ask you which gentleman of the midshipmen's berth conceived the idea of dicing instead of studying during the afternoon watch yesterday. I would only say that such procedure is not Duty.'

He paused.

'No, sir,' said Septimus.

'Nor,' continued the captain, still without turning, 'can I make any comment on Mr Pyke's action in sending you to the masthead during a gale. You understand that, I hope?'

'Yes, sir,' said Septimus.

'But I *do* propose,' went on his superior officer, 'to congratulate you on a brave and seamanlike piece of work, Mr Quinn.'

Captain Sainsbury swung round suddenly to face his junior midshipman. His stern face was lighted by the first smile Septimus had ever seen there.

'Mr Quinn,' he said, 'I think that some day we shall make a sea officer of you. That is all.'

'Aye aye, sir!' said Mr Midshipman Quinn.

Chapter Three

The Coward

I

Out of the flat blue of the Mediterranean rose a sunlit yellow cliff a thousand feet high, so mighty a precipice that the frigate moving past its base with her dazzling white sails spread looked like a tiny toy. Gibraltar. The guardian fortress of a great sea two thousand miles long whose coastline was all in the powerful hands of Napoleon Bonaparte or trembling in fear of him.

Midshipman Quinn, standing at the rail of His Majesty's frigate *Althea* to watch the famous 'Rock' fall astern as she sailed eastward, smiled grimly to himself as he thought of Napoleon Bonaparte, dictator of all Europe, ruling a nation three times the size of Britain but quite unable to prevent a British frigate from entering that great sea – because that guardian fortress was not French or Spanish but British. He told this thought to Midshipman the Honourable Charles Barry, who was standing beside him.

'Boney would give his ears for Gib, I'll wager,' drawled Barry. 'And if it wasn't for us, Sep – the Navy – we couldn't keep Gib, you know. I wonder,' he added, glancing towards the quarterdeck where Captain Sainsbury and his First Lieutenant paced in conversation, 'I wonder what our orders are.'

Everyone aboard *Althea* – except her captain – had been wondering that ever since she left Portsmouth fourteen days ago.

'Cocker thinks we are to join Lord Nelson off Toulon,' said Septimus.

'That's because Fitz has set his heart on fighting under Nelson. He wants broadsides and cutlass-waving and plenty of – of blood and thunder.'

Charles Barry spoke the words lightly, but there was an odd note in his voice – almost as if he disliked saying them. Septimus Quinn glanced quickly at him. Since the junior midshipman's rescue of Tod Beamish in mid-air, Barry and he had got to know each other rather better. Fitzroy Cocker still treated Septimus as he considered a large senior midshipman ought to treat a small junior one – with scorn and insult – but Barry had conceived a sincere respect for the younger boy's courage. Septimus liked him in spite of his rather spiritless bearing and drawling speech, and he had discovered some time ago that Barry had some secret trouble on his mind.

Barry met his glance and looked away. Then he turned to gaze with worried eyes at his brother midshipman. They were as nearly alone as any two people could be in the confined space of a ship-of-war.

'See here, Sep,' he said in a low voice, 'I'd like to tell you something. I've been wanting to tell someone for a long time. I'm afraid.'

'Afraid?' repeated Septimus, half-wondering whether he was joking. 'And pray, Charles, what are you afraid of?'

'Fighting – death – wounds,' Barry said hurriedly. 'Oh, I know it's a deuced awful thing to confess, but it's true. I've kept it to myself until now, and I'm only telling you because I know you won't make fun of me. I don't know what to do about it.'

Mr Quinn groped in the pocket of his blue uniform coat and got out his spectacle-case. It was a habit he had when confronted with a serious problem, and he had hooked the steel-rimmed glasses over one ear before he realised what he was about and hastily put them back again.

'But, Charles,' he said, frowning, 'we have so far seen no fighting. You can't be afraid of something you've never seen.'

'Yes, you can. At least, I can. I'm a coward, Sep – that's what it amounts to. I lie awake at night sweating to think how I might behave when we go into action. I'm not like Fitz, looking forward to getting to grips with the French, you see.'

Septimus thought this out for a moment. Then he looked up to nod reassuringly at his friend.

'In short, Charles,' he said in that grave manner which Fitzroy Cocker and Lieutenant George Pyke found so infuriating, 'you are afraid – of *being* afraid. That doesn't make you a coward. Pray don't distress yourself by thinking along those lines. When the time for action comes I shall be quite as nervous as you, I assure you. The only thing to do—'

His sage advice was cut short by the lusty squealing of the bosun's pipes calling *All hands*!

As he trotted aft towards the quarterdeck, with the barefooted seamen scurrying past him to form their divisions, Septimus was still frowning. He was troubled about his friend's confession.

Captain Sainsbury stood erect with hands linked behind him, looking down at the rows of brown faces in front of him. Every officer and man of the *Althea*'s complement of two hundred was waiting to hear what he had to say, except the few who could not be spared from the handling of the frigate. He raised his harsh voice so that it carried to the rearmost man.

'I want you all to understand that the Navy has many tasks to perform. We have been given a special task. It is unlikely to bring us much glory, and we may not take a single prize. This vessel is ordered to cruise independently along the French coast between Port Vendres and the Hyères Islands, with the object of bringing back information about the disposition of French forces along that coast.'

He paused. A slight rustle of movement ran along the ranks of seamen – hardly to be called a whispering, for no one spoke. It was the only sign of their disappointment.

'In the course of this main task,' resumed Captain Sainsbury as gravely as ever, 'we shall be forced to maintain close contact with the coast, along which a number of vessels – enemy vessels – are still plying their trade. It would not, I am sure, be the intention of Their Lordships at the Admiralty that these vessels should be allowed to reach their destination if we fall in with them.'

Again he paused, and this time the brown faces were grinning and here and there a deep chuckle sounded as someone tumbled to it that there would, after all, be enemy ships to capture and booty to be won. Midshipman Barry did not look particularly happy as he returned Midshipman Quinn's surreptitious wink.

'However,' the captain was saying, 'we shall not allow the chances of prize-taking to distract us from our duty, which is to discover all we can about Bonaparte's defences. That will mean landing-parties in enemy territory. We shall be striking a very harmful blow at the Frogs with every item of information we bring back, and if we can also find opportunity to destroy some of Boney's property – well, we'll not waste that opportunity.'

The men were all grinning widely now, and a voice piped up: 'Good old Saint! That's the med'cine for Boney!'

'I will flog the next man that raises his voice without orders,' said Captain Sainsbury without altering a muscle of his lean face. 'Ours is no easy task, and without proper discipline we shall not carry it through. I rely on every officer and man to do his duty. Mr Pyke, you may dismiss the men to their quarters.'

Pyke's bull voice roared the dismissal. Septimus and Charles Barry went down to the midshipmen's berth, where they found Mr Midshipman Cocker preparing to go on deck for signal duty on the quarterdeck. Beneath his red hair the face of the big senior midshipman was sullen.

'Well, Fitz,' Barry greeted him, 'you heard our fate, I presume? Lord Nelson isn't to have the honour of our company after all.'

'The worse for us, demme!' Cocker burst out, ramming his hat on defiantly. 'Prowling along the coast, snapping up defenceless trading-ships – where's the glory in that?'

'Nevertheless,' remarked Septimus mildly, 'our cruise may be a good deal more useful to England than half-a-dozen single-ship engagements.'

'Pah! May be – and may be not!' Fitzroy Cocker strode angrily towards the companion-ladder. At the foot of it he paused, ducking his head under the low deck-beams, to glare back at them. 'It's my belief,' he growled, 'that you're glad there's a chance of saving your precious skin, young lickspittle – you too, Charles!'

He ran up the ladder. Charles Barry, whose face had flushed dark red, turned to Septimus.

'What d'you think he meant by that?' he demanded. 'Sep, suppose he knows how I feel! Suppose he starts spreading the tale that I'm—'

'Pray don't distress yourself, Charles,' interrupted the junior midshipman. 'Our friend Fitz has the habit of speaking without thought. Just now he is angry and disappointed. His words meant nothing.'

But Barry would not be reassured. His fear of being a coward was beginning to prey on his nerves, Septimus reflected. The sooner Charles Barry had a chance of proving to himself that he could conquer fear, the better.

It was to be several days before that chance came. The *Althea* sailed steadily over the blue sea-miles of the Mediterranean with a favourable wind to speed her, keeping the coast of Spain just out of sight on her larboard beam. Spain, although she was in league with the Dictator of Europe, was not actively at war with Britain, and when (as happened twice) the frigate sighted a Spanish ship she merely displayed her colours and held on her course.

Those few days were not spent idly on board the *Althea*. The gun-crews were continually exercised under the supervision of Lieutenant Gifford, the second officer. The sails and rigging were overhauled piece by piece. Lieutenant Pyke exercised the seamen aloft whenever he got the chance, and the midshipmen were in turn put in charge of boat-lowering practice under conditions of absolute silence. Mr Pyke had not been as active in finding fault with Septimus since the midshipman's rescue of Tod Beamish. His red face still wore a scowl whenever his eye fell on Mr Quinn, however. Septimus suspected that Captain Sainsbury had spoken to the First Lieutenant about the unwisdom of sending junior midshipmen to the masthead during a gale, and he realised that if this was so he would be even less popular with Mr Pyke than before. 'Lobsterface' was the sort of man who would bear a grudge even against a boy of half his own age.

Young Mr Quinn did not let this worry him. The summer days at sea in the blue Mediterranean, and the prospect of excitement to come, kept him reasonably happy. It was on the fourth day after leaving Gibraltar that he became aware of a certain tenseness in the manner of everyone on board the *Althea*. The frigate had passed the latitude of the Pyrenees, and was entering the Gulf of Lions. No longer was there a neutral shore on her beam – she was cruising off the south coast of France, the arch-enemy of England, and gradually closing in towards enemy territory.

That night, an hour after sunset, Gifford, the Second Lieutenant, put his round pleasant face into the gunroom where the three midshipmen had just finished their supper.

'You're wanted in the main cabin, gentlemen,' he said with a smile. 'The captain's called a conference – and I think it'll be a council of war.'

The main cabin was in the extreme stern of the ship, not a very large room but a well-lit one, for a wide stern-window with lockers under it looked out above the big wooden rudder. Tonight it was lit by a large oil-lamp swinging from the low beams overhead. Captain Sainsbury and his three lieutenants were seated at the small table, and the midshipmen sat on the lockers in the window. The captain, as usual, wasted no time in preliminaries.

'We are about to commence operations, gentlemen,' he said, looking round the six intent faces. 'Port Vendres, and the town of Perpignan further inland, are just over the horizon. It is almost certain that the French have garrisons in both places and there may be ships of war in Port Vendres harbour. I wish to find out for certain.'

He flattened out a large chart that lay on the table in front of him, and beckoned the midshipmen to come forward so that they could see it.

'This curve of coast is all sandy beach,' he explained. 'Here is Port Vendres, strongly fortified. The guns of that fort will be twenty-pounders at least – probably heavier. We cannot hope to get near the port without being observed and blown out of the water before our own guns are in range. Here – ten miles to the north and inland from the coast – you see Perpignan, a large fortified town. Our map is incomplete, but there must be a road connecting the two. Probably it runs along the coast some little distance from the shore. There will be a considerable amount of traffic along that road between two fortified towns.'

He leaned back from the chart and once more looked at his officers.

'I want prisoners,' he continued. 'At the same time, I wish to try and keep *Althea*'s presence on this coast from becoming known to the French. I have called you all to this council, but only three officers will be needed for this landing operation, which will be a small one.'

'I wish to volunteer,' barked Lieutenant Pyke at once.

'Thank you, Mr Pyke. I must ask you, however, to let me choose on this occasion. Mr Gifford will command the whole operation, for which I shall send the launch and the cutter. Mr Barry will be in command of the launch, with Mr Quinn to second him.'

He looked up inquiringly as a muffled sound between a snort and a gurgle came from Midshipman Cocker, but that young gentleman was sitting with his mouth tightly shut and an expression of angry disappointment on his face. The captain went on with his explanation.

'I shall leave the details of organisation to Mr Gifford, but I want these orders observed. One of the two boats is to land two miles north of Port Vendres, the other two miles south of the mouth of the River Tet, on which Perpignan stands. The landings will thus be about six miles apart along the coast. The boats will put off tomorrow night from *Althea*, who will stand by six miles offshore. Since I wish to keep the frigate below the horizon, I shall not be able to support the landings. Is that clear?'

Lieutenant Gifford leaned forward. 'I take it, sir,' he said, 'that our best plan will be to get into position near the road before dawn, and then—'

'You are in command, Mr Gifford,' interrupted Captain Sainsbury. 'How you capture your men is your business. I suggest, however, that each party should bring back one prisoner only, and that such prisoner should if possible be a man who can tell us something about the military situation ashore. You will remember that army patrols and convoys use that road. I rely on your proved discretion to avoid any fighting, of course. But if you find it possible to take a French officer – well, that might be worth a skirmish.'

2

At three o'clock in the morning, thirty-one hours after Captain Sainsbury had issued his preliminary orders, two boats in line ahead were creeping in towards the French coast. The night was moonless, and the glimmer of stars showed the two black shapes like many-legged beetles. A faint glow of phosphorescence showed each time the oars dipped their blades, but there was no creaking from the muffled rowlocks.

A light breeze had enabled both boats to make the better part of their six-mile voyage under sail. Before the low broken line of the coast had appeared, however, Mr Gifford had ordered sail in and masts lowered and they had taken to the oars. The cutter was in the lead. Astern of her followed the launch, with Charles Barry at the tiller and Septimus Quinn sitting in the sternsheets beside him. Both had cutlasses at their sides, as had the nine seamen in their boat. Pistols had not been issued, for silence was an essential part of their plan even if they had to beat off an attack.

'Can't be far off the shore now,' muttered Barry nervously.

'Mr Gifford will give us the word,' replied Septimus reassuringly.

He could feel the slight trembling of Barry's arm. He repressed a wish that he, and not his friend, had been given command of a boat – Charles was so plainly unsure of himself. But Septimus was bound to obey any orders Charles might give, not because he was a year younger but because his name was further down the List at the Admiralty. It was the law of the Navy. When two officers of equal rank were together, the one who had joined first, and whose name was therefore higher on the List, was the senior of the two.

'Cutter's stopped pulling,' said Barry suddenly. ' 'Vast pulling, launch.'

The launch crept alongside the leading boat, and Lieutenant Gifford's voice came across the intervening space of dark water.

'We're about a mile offshore, Mr Barry. We'll part here. If my reckoning's correct, we're midway between our landing-points. You know your course?'

'North by west, sir.'

'Yes. I'd keep a little north of that. You'll pull five knots, roughly, so if you row for thirty-five minutes and then head in for the shore you'll be in position. Good luck!'

'Aye aye, sir. Good luck to you!'

The cutter's head bore away and she disappeared into the night as the launch turned in the opposite direction and began to move northward.

Most of the previous day had been spent in discussing and preparing the operation, for though it was a small one and likely to be straightforward if all went well, nothing could be left to chance except the actual taking of prisoners. Midshipmen Barry and Quinn knew exactly what they had to do by the time they had finished discussing it with Lieutenant Gifford. They were to land with eight men, leaving the ninth in charge of the boat. Then they were to find the coast road – without being observed – and wait in ambush according to what facilities the roadside offered for concealment. If and when they secured a prisoner, they were to make their way back to the ship independently of Gifford's party. Every effort was to be made to avoid leading the enemy to the beach or otherwise giving away the presence of a British ship.

Tod Beamish (who made one of the launch's crew) carried a small bag slung round his shoulders containing two carefully prepared gags and several short lengths of line for binding the prisoner. Septimus had added an idea of his own by getting the gunner's mate to provide him with a narrow canvas sleeve eighteen inches long and three inches wide. When Mr Preece asked him what it was for, he replied that prisoners might make a lot of noise even if they were gagged, which made Mr Preece scratch his grizzled head in bewilderment.

Steadily northward crept the launch, and soon the slightly uneven black line that was the coast began to stand out more sharply against the stars. On their starboard hand the eastern sky was paling when Barry, kneeling in the bottom of the boat and striking flint and steel under cover of his coat, looked at his watch.

'Another three minutes,' he announced in a shaky whisper. 'Keep pulling, men – and no talking from now on.'

The dark shape of the launch moved on for a short distance and then Barry put the tiller over and she headed straight in for the shore. In five minutes they could hear the sound of waves breaking on a beach.

'Not much of a surf,' whispered Midshipman Quinn. 'We could ground bows-on. It's not likely we'll find anyone about for miles.'

'Unless the French have had warning of us,' returned Barry uneasily. 'In that case, they may be there – waiting for us.'

'Here are the breakers,' said Septimus quickly. 'Watch your helm, Charles!'

The launch rose on a wavecrest and the white of the surf could be seen ahead. The two bowmen shipped their oars, ready to leap out and drag her bows up the beach when she grounded. Ten strokes, and the keel grated on small shingle. Thirty seconds later the British landing-party was standing on French ground.

'I thought I heard a – a voice,' quavered Barry, peering round him in the darkness. He was gripping Midshipman Quinn's arm tightly. 'Perhaps it'd be wiser to pull off again and listen.'

'Steady, Charles,' Septimus whispered urgently in his friend's ear. 'The beach is deserted. Better tell Hubbard to keep the launch well offshore until we return, in case anyone comes along.

Barry pulled himself together and gave the order. The launch with her crew of one was shoved off, and the eight men clustered round the two midshipmen ready for further orders. Barry, who was obviously suffering from nervousness, said nothing, and Septimus realised that he would have to take action himself – his senior was for the moment incapable of it.

'If I remember correctly, Mr Barry,' he said in a low voice that the men could could hear, 'you decided that I should lead the file, as my sight in the dark is better than yours.'

'Yes – yes, of course,' said Barry hastily. 'Pray lead the way, Sep – I mean Mr Quinn. I will bring up the rear.'

'Aye aye,' returned Septimus. 'Single file, then – every man close up to his leader – no noise. Follow me.'

He started up the gentle slope of the shingle. It was impossible to avoid making a noise in crossing it, but soon they came to soft sand with stunted bushes growing here and there and a line of low trees beyond. A small square shape appeared among the trees. Septimus halted the file and went to speak to Barry.

'There's a building in front,' he whispered. 'I suggest I go on to reconnoitre while you wait here.

'If it's a farm,' Charles whispered back, 'couldn't we kidnap the farmer and run for it?'

'He wouldn't be the sort of prisoner the captain wants, I fear. I'll go and see where we are.'

Without waiting for Barry's agreement, he ran forward. The dawn would soon be here and there was no time to waste.

The line of trees bordered a vineyard, he found, and the square shape was a stone building that seemed deserted. He trotted noiselessly along the edge of the vineyard, thinking what a pity it was that Charles Barry was unable to feel this thrill of excitement at prowling into Bonaparte's territory – territory where discovery would mean death or imprisonment. Septimus had to admit that his friend was showing himself a coward indeed. But he was not convinced that cowardice was part of Barry's character. If only he could make Barry see himself as he really was, force him to prove himself capable of courage in the face of the enemy – and Septimus believed that he *was* capable of it – he might save his friend

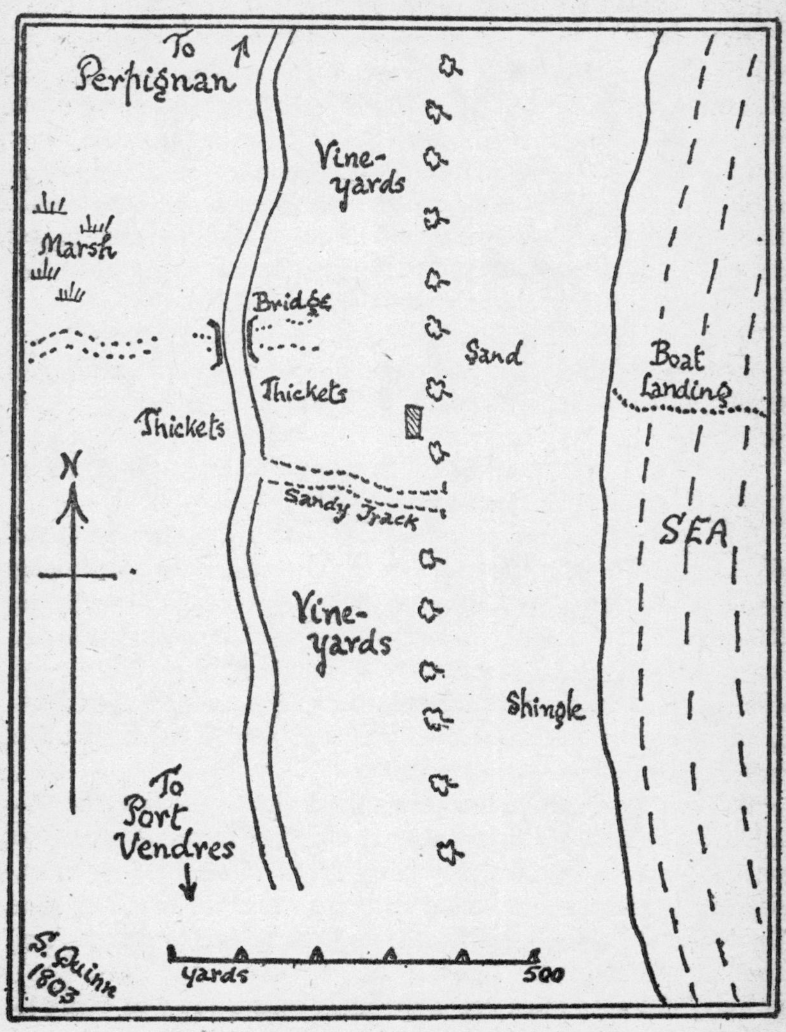

Part of the Coast of France, with the Place where we landed and took a Prisoner.
From Midshipman Quinn's private Log.

from disgrace. But in the midst of a perilous night operation there seemed little chance of scheming for such an occasion.

Here was a gap in the line of trees. A sandy track divided one big vineyard from another, it appeared, and the track was heading directly away from the beach. It was bound to lead to the coast road – if there was one – because the vine harvesters would want to take their produce to market in Perpignan by cart. He need go no further with his reconnaissance. As he turned away, Septimus remembered that the grapes would be nearly ripe. He went to the nearest vine-tree and plucked the biggest bunch he could feel in the darkness, before scuttling back the way he had come.

When he felt soft sand under his feet he paused again, to fill the canvas sleeve Mr Preece had made him. A minute later he was tossing his captured grapes to the seamen, who sucked them thirstily.

'Spoils of war,' he said. 'All is clear, Mr Barry. If you will follow, I can bring you to the coast road.'

The party of ten, in single file, moved silently to the edge of the vineyard and came to the sandy track. Three hundred paces along it brought them within a few yards of its end, where it appeared to join another track. Again Septimus went on alone, moving silently at the very edge of the track. At the junction his suspicions were confirmed. A wide metalled road, obviously a main road of some importance, ran north and south bordered by trees and bushes. He went back and reported this to Barry.

'We can rig an ambush within a short distance of this lane,' he added. 'I suggest, Mr Barry, that we take four men each and hide ourselves on the roadside, my party fifty feet from yours. Then, supposing a Frenchman comes along from my direction, I let him pass – you stop him – and I come up from behind to prevent him from escaping.'

Barry did not at first reply, probably because he was trying to stop the chattering of his teeth.

'W-would it not be b-better to wait in the lane here?' he suggested at last.

The darkness hid the sharp dig in the ribs which Septimus

administered, and he took care that the seamen did not hear his whispered *'Pull yourself together!'*

'I fancy the road myself,' he said aloud. 'And we had better get into position quickly if you agree.'

Barry seemed to make an effort, and spoke with some decision.

'Very well, then. And we take the first chance we get, and rush our prisoner away down the lane.'

Septimus would have liked to say that it would be better to let the first passer-by go free unless he looked like being useful, but he decided that he could not, this time, question Barry's order.

'I'll take Beamish, Rudd, Tipper, and Garraway,' he said, since his senior had again fallen into uneasy silence. 'Come on, men.'

They went forward into the road and Septimus turned to the right along it. He led the way past a stone bridge which crossed a dry stream-bed, and stopped by a thick fringe of bushes. His eyes were well used to the darkness by now, and he could make out the other five halting twenty paces further back and watch them disappear into the roadside thickets. He led his own men into the bushes and told them to make themselves comfortable.

'If you want to scratch yourselves or break twigs,' he added, 'do it now. And give Beamish plenty of room. I want to listen without any noise from you.'

Hoarse chuckles and a chorus of whispered 'Aye-ayes' answered him. He settled himself behind a low thorn-bush close to the roadside and prepared to wait.

The stars winked down through the twigs over his head – there was no sign of daybreak there. The 'false dawn' that had appeared earlier had not spread over the sky. It would be hard luck, he told himself, if no one came along that road before sunrise, but the attempt would still have to be made. The minutes lengthened out into what seemed like hours, and his straining ears had picked up no sound except the distant murmur of the sea and the occasional high note of an insect. Some sort of stinging fly was bothering the men, and he had to whisper a sharp reprimand when someone let out a hoarse oath. He had scarcely done so when the sound of a man's voice singing reached him.

The seamen heard it too, and crouched in absolute silence. The singing came nearer, and footsteps could now be heard – footsteps as unsteady as the singing. They were approaching from northward, the direction of Perpignan, and would pass the lair of Septimus and his men before reaching Barry's ambush.

Cautiously Septimus poked out his head so that he could look along the road. A dark figure was already in sight, not more than thirty yards away, stumbling along drunkenly. A French farmhand, probably, reeling home after a night's wine-bibbing with his friends in Perpignan. The information that such a man could give wouldn't be much use to a British frigate, thought Midshipman Quinn as the man shambled past only a foot or two from him, raucously singing

'Auprès de ma blonde,
Qu'il fait bon, fait bon, fait bon,
Auprès de ma blonde,
Qu'il fait—'

The singing stopped abruptly, and simultaneously Septimus and his party ran out on to the road. They were in time to see Barry and his four men make an easy capture. The dazed and bewildered labourer – for such he seemed to be – made no resistance and was allowed to make no noise. Brawny arms held him while he was neatly gagged and his hands tied behind him.

'Got him!' Barry said triumphantly as Septimus came up to him. 'Now for the shore and back on board!'

'Wait,' Septimus begged him urgently. 'You speak good French, Charles, don't you? Better than mine?'

'I suppose so,' replied Barry with obvious impatience. 'But why—'

'Listen, Charles. It's just possible we can do better than this fellow.'

'I'm not going to wait,' said Barry nervously. 'A cavalry patrol might come along this road any moment.'

'Two minutes won't make much difference.' Septimus drew his

friend away from the group of men. 'All I suggest is that you get the party off the road – into the stream-bed by that bridge, if you like – and ask this fellow a few questions.'

'But—'

'Pray do as I ask, Charles. Under the bridge we'll be hidden from anyone who passes on the road.'

Barry hesitated and then gave in, though he plainly disliked the idea. The seamen pulled their grunting prisoner down the bank of the dried-up stream and into the black shadows of the bridge. The two midshipmen followed.

'Now, Mr Barry,' said Septimus, drawing the cutlass from his belt, 'if Beamish takes off that gag, I venture to suggest our prisoner may be able to tell you something of interest. But first, tell him that if he makes any sound above a whisper, I'll cut his throat.'

As he spoke he let the point of his weapon rest against the neck of the Frenchman, who squirmed away from it. Barry, whose French was a good deal more fluent than Septimus's, did as he suggested. The gag was taken out, and the prisoner's first choking protests silenced by a gentle pressure of the cutlass-point.

'Ask him if any soldiers pass along this road,' muttered Septimus.

Barry repeated it in French. The prisoner, evidently partly sobered by the shock of his capture, replied without hesitation that soldiers did pass, every day. They took supplies from Perpignan to the garrison at Port Vendres. No, he didn't know how many soldiers there were in either town. But he could tell them that there was a big French ship-of-war, the *Vengeur*, in Port Vendres harbour.

'Is this road patrolled by soldiers?'

Why, of course it was. It was the main coast road, and there were patrols on it day and night, cavalry patrols of twenty men and a sergeant. Prompted by Septimus, Barry asked when the night patrol usually passed that spot. And the answer made both midshipmen jump.

'At this time, *messieurs*, coming from Perpignan. I am surprised it has not passed already.'

3

'I tell you, Charles, it's our duty,' whispered Septimus urgently.

'I won't do it – we must get away at once,' Charles Barry returned, trying to pull his arm from the other's grasp.

'You must see that this prisoner's not much use. He knows nothing about the garrisons. He says there's a sergeant in command of these patrols of dragoons, and that's the man we want. Quick, Charles – it depends on you.'

Septimus had dragged his friend a short distance away from the others to pour into his ear a brief outline of the plan he proposed. Charles was required to play a leading part in this plan, for he alone could speak French well enough to sound like a Frenchman. He had refused vehemently, but the young midshipman could tell that it was only fear of losing his nerve that was keeping Charles Barry from taking a chance.

At any moment the sound of hoofbeats on the road from Perpignan might tell them that it was too late. Septimus played his last card.

'If you're coward enough to refuse, Charles,' he said between his teeth, 'pray stand aside. I'll do it for you.'

'You can't!' gasped Barry in dismay. 'They'll know you're English the moment you say a word!'

'I don't care. I shall do it.'

'See here, Sep – this is mutiny,' muttered Barry. 'If I report you—'

'Report me, then. It will be worth it. Stand aside, please!'

Barry drew a long breath.

'All right,' he said desperately. 'I'll try it. But—'

'Good,' snapped Midshipman Quinn briefly. 'I'll see to the placing of the men. Remember – straight under the bridge when we've got him.'

He raced back to the others without waiting for Barry's reply. The dawn light was growing now, and he could see that the gag was back in their first prisoner's mouth and his ankles tied together. The Frenchman would have to be left there – no doubt someone would find him next day.

'Mr Barry's party!' he said briskly. 'All of you except – who's the tallest? – Pierce, into the thicket west of the road, twenty paces north of this bridge. Wait there until you hear me screech at the top of my voice – I've a good screech – and then rush out and lay on with your cutlasses. Use the flats, and hit all the horses you can. I want real confusion, but no shouting, mind. When you hear me screech a second time, make westward into these thickets with as much noise as you can. To your action-stations, now!'

As the three seamen crept across the road and disappeared into the shadowy bushes, he turned to his own four men.

'Beamish, you and Pierce will come with me. The rest of you heard what I told Mr Barry's party? Good. You'll hide in the bushes opposite them. Do exactly as they do. Garraway, take charge of the diversion party and bring every man to the beach when the action's over. Carry on!'

With Pierce and Beamish at his heels, he hurried to where Barry was standing irresolutely at the roadside. Already, he noticed, it was light enough to see the dead whiteness of Charles's face.

'All's ready, Mr Barry,' he reported formally.

Charles grasped the midshipman's arm with a shaking hand.

'Sep!' he whispered hoarsely. 'I can't—'

'*Listen!*'

In the silence that followed the tense exclamation the distant clatter of approaching hoofbeats came clearly to their ears. A troop of horsemen were cantering towards them from the direction of Perpignan.

'Here they come,' remarked Septimus calmly. His hand closed on Charles's shoulder for a second. 'We all depend on you, Mr Barry.'

With that, he stepped from the roadway into the cover of a clump of leafy bushes. Beamish and Pierce joined him there. From their shelter they could see the road's pale glimmer under the paling sky, and Charles Barry's solitary figure standing motionless. And the hoofbeats came nearer.

Mr Midshipman Quinn, it must be admitted, felt a certain nervousness himself as he waited there in the dim twilight of early morning. He knew quite well that his plan was a daring one, and that if Barry failed them the plan would fail. He, Septimus Quinn, would be responsible for its failure then. He might be killed or taken prisoner. If he escaped, he would have to report that he had forced a senior officer to adopt a futile scheme against his will – and that might mean a Court Martial and disgrace. But if Barry played his part there was, he thought, a good chance of the plan succeeding. And more would be gained than a valuable prisoner. Charles Barry would have been cured of cowardice.

The horsemen were so close now that he could hear the jingle of accoutrements. He looked at Barry's shadowy figure again. It had not moved. One English midshipman had to nerve himself to face twenty French dragoons, to risk discovery and almost certain death. Barry had only to step back into the bushes, letting the oncoming troop sweep past, to escape the test. Would he stand firm? Could he carry it through?

Septimus in his anxiety was squeezing the sand-filled canvas sleeve he carried. Between the leaves of his bush he saw the massed horsemen coming, the growing light gleaming dully on their polished helmets. They were almost at the bridge – their hoofbeats drummed upon it. And then Midshipman the Honourable Charles Barry did the bravest thing of his life. He stepped out into the roadway.

'Halte-là!'

His voice rang loudly and with authority. The leader of the dragoon patrol shouted at his men and they reined in their horses. Barry took a step forward.

'I have orders for the sergeant-in-charge,' he said in French, haughtily.

The leader of the troop edged his horse a little forward.

'I am he, monsieur,' he answered gruffly. 'May I ask what authority you have for stopping—'

Septimus waited no longer. He raised his voice in an earsplitting screech, and dashed out of cover with the two tall seamen close behind him. Simultaneously, pandemonium broke loose on the dark road.

Out from the bushes behind the dragoons broke half-a-dozen seamen, to rush in among the horses smiting left and right with the flattened blades of their cutlasses. Frightened horses squealed and reared, men roared French oaths, the twenty dragoons became a milling mob of horsemen cannoning into each other and trying to control their mounts. Not a man of them had time to notice what was happening to their sergeant.

Septimus's rush had brought him to the bridle of the leader's horse. Charles dashed to seize it from the other side. The gigantic Beamish, aided by the equally tall Pierce, flung themselves at the rider and plucked him from his saddle like a ripe fruit. Before the dragoons had realised that there were armed enemies among them, the hapless sergeant was hauled down the bank and under the bridge. His one shout for help was drowned in the general uproar, and a second later Midshipman Quinn's loaded sandbag had descended on the back of his head. The sergeant lay still. Then, piercing as ever but sounding oddly far away, that eldritch screech rose again.

Under the bridge crouched the four sailors with their unconscious victim. This was the dangerous moment, as Septimus knew. If anyone had seen their silent rush to cover, if anyone had realised that the second screech had come from under the bridge, they were doomed. He heard above the tumult of plunging horses a new sound – a hoarse yelling and crashing in the thickets west of the road, going further away. And he heard the furious shouts of the dragoons. One of them was shouting to his comrades to follow – that the cursed bandits had run into the bushes. The cry was taken up. The dragoons were spurring their horses in pursuit, screaming for vengeance as they rode. Garraway and his men had done their work well.

Septimus waited until the last horseman had left the road and then peered over the parapet of the bridge. The coast was clear.

Beamish slung the unconscious sergeant over his shoulders like a sack of meal and the four sped across the road and down the sandy lane to the beach. The long line of the sea was clear-cut against the glorious colours of the dawn sky, and there, creeping inshore to meet them, was their waiting boat.

It was nearly ten minutes – an anxious ten minutes – before Garraway and his men came stumbling down the shingle. They were all breathless, and black with mud to the thighs.

'The dragoons aren't following?' remanded Septimus sharply.

'N-not they, sir,' panted Garraway. He and the others were grinning widely despite their tired state. 'There was a bog t'other side them thickets, sir – we led 'em into that, and I doubt if they'll ever get out.'

Septimus turned to Barry. 'A very successful venture, Mr Barry,' he remarked.

Charles Barry drew himself erect. There was a new light in his eye and a new tone in his voice.

'It succeeded because every man here did his duty,' he said clearly. 'We mustn't be caught now, men. Into the launch, and back to the old *Althea* for breakfast.'

4

The morning sunlight streamed through the stern window into the main cabin where Captain Sainsbury was receiving the reports of his landing-party officers.

'You'll be glad to hear, gentlemen,' he said, 'that the two prisoners you brought in have given me most valuable information. Mr Gifford captured a Port Vendres fisherman, who was able to inform me that the French line-of-battle ship *Vengeur*, twice the *Althea*'s strength, is lying in Port Vendres harbour ready for sea.'

'Midshipman Quinn and Midshipman Barry exchanged rapid winks. They had obtained most of this information themselves.

'That is a fact well worth knowing, both for our own safety and for the information of Lord Nelson,' continued the captain. 'As for the sergeant of dragoons captured by the party commanded by Mr Barry, he was more helpful still. He proves to have secret royalist sympathies and has told everything he knows, which is a good deal. We know the strength of the garrisons in both Port Vendres and Perpignan, and the sergeant has given a most illuminating account of the French Army patrol system between here and Marseilles and of the aid given by Spain to these southern garrisons. You took a most valuable prisoner, Mr Barry.'

Coming from Captain Sainsbury, this was high commendation, and Charles Barry reddened with pleasure. He could not let it pass, though.

'By your leave, sir,' he said, 'the whole plan for capturing the dragoon sergeant was the work of Mr Quinn. It was he who persuaded me—'

'Not at all, sir,' broke in Septimus quickly. 'Mr Barry was in command, and took the leading part in the plan. He—'

'Pray allow me to speak, gentlemen,' interrupted the captain in his turn, frowning. 'I was about to add that although Mr Barry was fortunate in his prisoner, it appears that an unwarrantable risk was taken in obtaining him. In your report to Mr Gifford, Mr Barry, you state that a force of twenty French dragoons was halted on the main coast road by your party of eight seamen and thrown into confusion, thus allowing the sergeant to be kidnapped. You were in command, as Mr Quinn points out, and took the leading part. If your report is correct, you endangered your small force recklessly and risked the discovery of the *Althea*'s presence on this coast.'

'If you please, sir,' put in Septimus as he paused, 'I must admit to full responsibility for the plan. As Mr Barry says, I did persuade him to adopt it, against his own judgement—'

'Not a bit of it!' Charles said loudly. 'If anyone is to be blamed it's me. I was in command.'

He stopped as Captain Sainsbury held up his hand commandingly. Both midshipmen met the captain's gaze as it moved sternly from one to the other. The severe lines of their commanding officer's face relaxed a little.

'It seems,' he remarked, 'that you are unable to decide on a question of fact. The credit is disclaimed by both of you, the blame is taken by both of you. I shall say nothing more about the blame, except to comment' – here he looked straight at Septimus – 'that prudence, as well as zeal and ingenuity, is expected of a sea officer. Such good fortune will not always attend so daring a plan.'

He sat back in his chair and turned his level gaze on Charles Barry.

'As to the credit,' he continued, 'I will merely say that the whole party bore themselves well. But – however dark the night – to face twenty French dragoons alone and in uniform was a thing requiring considerable courage. The officer who did that, Mr Barry, was certainly no coward. That is all.'

Chapter Four

Pistols For Two

I

Midshipman Septimus Quinn peered through his spectacles at the chart which lay open on the table. On the opposite side of the table, which was in the dimly-lit gunroom of the frigate *Althea*, Senior Midshipman Fitzroy Cocker bent his fiery red head over the same chart as he toiled with dividers and parallel rulers to find the frigate's position.

'Deuce take it!' he muttered angrily to himself. 'That puts her about two miles inland!'

'You have probably not taken the compass variation into account,' suggested Septimus. 'The angle should—'

'When I want instruction from you I'll ask for it,' snapped Cocker, scowling at him.

Septimus raised his eyebrows and quietly continued his own calculations. Fitzroy Cocker had not troubled to conceal his scorn of the spectacled midshipman from the day Mr Quinn had joined the *Althea*, and recent events had by no means improved his temper. Cocker had been furious at being passed over when Septimus and Charles Barry had been chosen for the raiding-party, and the fact that the others had won considerable credit by bringing in a valuable prisoner had only increased his wrath. Furthermore, Charles was beginning to leave the hot-tempered Cocker alone and seek the company of the junior midshipman in their off-duty hours. Cocker never spoke to Septimus nowadays without a snarl or an insult.

Mr Midshipman Quinn, who had correctly located the *Althea*'s position ten miles south-west of the enemy port of Cette, gravely considered the case of himself and Fitzroy Cocker. The situation was becoming unbearable. In the confined space of a thirty-eight-gun frigate any friction between shipmates made life very uncomfortable. It was bad enough to have made an enemy of the frigate's First Lieutenant, but Mr Pyke only came into contact with Midshipman Quinn in the course of duty while Fitzroy Cocker was his messmate.

Septimus had come to no conclusion on this point, except that something would soon have to be done about it, when there was a squealing of pipes from the deck above, followed instantly by the stirring *rataplan* of the marines' drums and the shouting of rapid orders.

Without exchanging a word, the two midshipmen leapt to their feet, seized their hats, and hurried up the companion ladder to the deck. That drum-beat was 'Quarters!' It might mean that the frigate was going into action.

After the gloom of the cabin the sunlight on deck made them blink. It was a brilliantly sunny afternoon, and the incredible blue of the Mediterranean stretched on every side with only the light summer breeze to ruffle it and send the *Althea* steadily through the water under full sail. The deck was crowded with seamen scampering to their action stations and noisy with the rumble of guns being run out. Midshipman Charles Barry was on the quarterdeck, a little apart from the captain and his lieutenants. He beckoned excitedly to the two as they made their way towards him.

'We sighted two enemy sail five minutes ago,' he told them, 'and we're bearing down on them. There they are – starboard bow.'

The two ships were a couple of miles away across the blue sea, one of them rather larger than the *Althea* and the other smaller. They were heading away, but the frigate was slowly overhauling them.

'They're French,' said Barry, with an eye on Captain

Sainsbury, who was ordering the setting of studding-sails. 'The big one's a merchant ship, but the other's a sloop-of-war.'

'Then they may show fight, demme!' said Cocker. 'The merchantman's bound to be armed. By heaven, I hope we have a sea-fight!' He turned to grin unpleasantly at Septimus. 'That'll show young lickspittle his first bit of real war and test his little nerves.'

Barry, who was on duty as signal midshipman, had his spyglass to his eye. A rag of bunting had fluttered to the yardarm of both the distant vessels.

'French colours!' he exclaimed. 'And—' he broke off to report eagerly to the captain. 'The merchantman's got a big gun aft, sir – a twenty-four pounder, it might be.'

Captain Sainsbury nodded without taking his gaze from the enemy ships. 'Thank you, Mr Barry. I had observed it.' He shot one glance over his shoulder. 'Mr Cocker! Go for'ard to your station! Mr Quinn! Stand by here as messenger!'

'Aye aye, sir!' returned the midshipmen together, and Cocker hurried towards the foredeck at the double.

'The merchantman's low in the water and we're overhauling nicely,' Septimus heard the captain remark to Lieutenant Pyke. 'I'll have that cargo, whatever it is.'

The setting of the studding-sails, additional canvas hoisted at the sides of the frigate's ordinary sails, was making a difference to her speed. The ships ahead were visibly growing larger as the distance decreased.

'Almost within range, sir,' said Mr Gifford, the Second Lieutenant. He put his glass to his eye. 'There's activity round that big gun on the merchantman. I think—'

He stopped speaking as a puff of white smoke broke suddenly from the merchantman's stern. A second or two afterwards a loud splash several hundred feet astern of the frigate and well to one side showed that the shot had been badly aimed.

'Shall I open fire with the stern-chasers, sir?' ventured Gifford.

'No. I wish to reserve my fire for the sloop. She is out-gunned and we should deal with her easily. That twenty-four pounder won't hurt us if they do no better than that.'

As the captain finished speaking a second puff of white appeared from the merchantmen. This time, by luck or better judgement, the ball screamed through the rigging of the *Althea*'s foremast.

'Mr Quinn!' rapped the captain. 'For'ard with you and see what damage has been done.'

Septimus ran along the deck, between the rows of guns with their crews standing ready and stripped to the waist, and found Midshipman Cocker.

'Two topmast shrouds gone,' Cocker said briefly in reply to his question. He was staring at the sloop, now quite close ahead. 'Ah! Now you're going to stand fire, my lad. Look at that!'

The sloop had made a full turn to starboard, bringing the wind dead astern of her, and the line of her open gun-ports was presented to the pursuing frigate. As Septimus looked, that line vanished in a gush of smoke and orange flame. Then came the crash of the discharge, and immediately after it a high and terrifying screaming, approaching at lightning speed. Involuntarily Septimus ducked as the cannon-balls flew fifty feet overhead.

'Stand up, young lickspittle!' Cocker shouted, grinning contemptuously at him. 'This is different from skulking in the bushes ashore while Barry takes the risk – eh?'

'Mr Cocker,' returned the junior midshipman, looking him in the eye, 'I shall remember that insult.'

'Oh, go to blazes!' snapped the other, turning away to stare up at the sails. 'Or better still, report to Captain Sainsbury that the broadside did no damage. Look sharp, now!'

Septimus obeyed immediately. But as he hurried aft he made a resolution that Cocker's scornful animosity should be brought to an end one way or another. And there was only one way to put an end to repeated insult.

Lieutenant Gifford came running from the quarterdeck as Septimus approached it. He passed the midshipman without looking at him, and a second later his voice rang out.

'Starboard gun-crews, stand by!'

Captain Sainsbury roared an order, the frigate spun round with a cracking of canvas, and Gifford's yell of '*Fire*!' followed almost at once. Septimus was nearly flung over as the *Althea* heeled with the shock of her broadside. He recovered himself and made for where the captain was standing. But Captain Sainsbury was too busy for the moment to receive a report. He was peering into the great drifting cloud of smoke, waiting eagerly for it to blow aside and give a view of the sloop against which eighteen guns had roared destruction. A gap appeared, and in it the sloop could be seen. At first it looked as though she had suffered no damage. And then Septimus, staring hard through the remnants of smoke, saw that nearly the whole length of her larboard rail had been blown away. There was no sign of damage to masts or sails, however, and she did not stop to await a second broadside. With a freshening breeze filling her canvas, she fled away from her charge the merchantman.

'The white-livered Frogs!' jeered Lieutenant Pyke. 'Deserting their duty, begad!'

'Small blame to them, sir,' rejoined the captain tartly. 'They did well to stand our fire, being no match for our weight. Have a boarding-party ready for the other, Mr Pyke, if you please. Take Mr Haswell and Mr Cocker.'

'Aye aye, sir!'

Pyke strode for'ard, shouting orders. The frigate was holding her course for the merchant ship now. Her destined victim was heavily laden and sailing slowly. But it seemed that there were Frenchmen of spirit on board her, for the big twenty-four pounder spoke for the third time at short range. There was a crash aloft, and a chorus of shouts. The frigate's fore-topmast had been hit and shattered. Down came topsail and rigging in a great tangle, and huge splinters and shafts of wood from the wrecked mast smashed to the deck, killing one seaman and wounding two more.

A party headed by the ship's carpenter sprang to clear the wreckage, but even the loss of the topsail did not appear to slow the *Althea*'s speed perceptibly. She was coming up fast on the merchantman's quarter, and the latter's big gun would no longer bear. Septimus, his report forgotten and now hardly necessary, watched with a thrill of excitement as the pursuing warship closed upon her quarry. Closer and closer came the big vessel, until he could see the red caps of the men on board – then their brown faces. Suddenly there was only a few yards of water between the two gliding hulls. A grinding shock made the frigate shudder from stem to stern. Grappling-hooks hurtled through the air from the British ship, drawing the vessels close together. With a cheer Lieutenant Pyke and his boarding-party surged over the locked bulwarks on to the Frenchman's deck.

There was only a short resistance, as might have been expected. Within five minutes the *Marie-Lepenseur* of Cette had struck her colours and her crew were prisoners. The sloop was already a white speck on the northern horizon.

The *Marie-Lepenseur* turned out to be a disappointing prize. She carried a cargo of hides – hides and nothing else – and though hides were doubtless valuable to the French they were of little use to a British frigate. Captain Sainsbury had to decide whether to destroy her or to put a prize crew on board, and his decision was for destruction. He had a mission to fulfil and could spare no men at this early stage of it. The French crew and their captain were put in their ship's boats with food and water and ordered to pull for the coast. Then the *Marie-Lepenseur* was set on fire and the *Althea* sailed away from her as fast as she could. For one thing, that column of black smoke could be seen for miles, and might bring French warships out to investigate. And for another, the burning hides stank horribly.

There was a good deal of work to be done by everyone on board the frigate, and the midshipmen had their share of it. The tangle of gear on the foremast had to be cleared, a jury topmast hoisted and rigged, and every detail of decks and rigging made shipshape and in perfect readiness for battle before there was rest for the *Althea*'s officers and crew. It was well after sunset when Captain Sainsbury, sitting in his cabin to write the necessary report on the action with sloop and merchantman, received a tale of woe from Roberts, the ship's carpenter.

'Didn't find out about it, sir, until we got the biggest part of the topmast out of the forehatch,' he explained apologetically. 'Sheer bad luck it was, the mast finding that one place. If it'd only come down some other place—'

'Come to the point, man!' broke in the captain impatiently. 'What happened? Was anyone hurt?'

'No, sir, no. It was the water supply. Three of the big casks was smashed by the falling mast and another sprung a leak.'

'I see.' Sainsbury stroked his chin. 'That means we've water for three days only. Very good, Roberts. My compliments to Mr Pyke and I wish to speak with him at once.'

The loss of the water was a serious thing indeed. Cruising as she was off a long hostile coast, with no friendly port into which she could put for supplies and no friendly vessel nearer than Toulon, 120 miles away, the frigate had to be self-supporting. She had carried an extra supply of water, already only drinkable by mixing it with wine or lime-juice, but that was now gone. It was essential to take in fresh supplies if she was to continue on her solitary mission.

The result of Captain Sainsbury's discussion with his First Lieutenant was that the frigate altered course and headed north-north-east. This was naturally commented on by all her crew and the news of the captain's intention quickly spread. Mr Preece, the old Welsh gunner's mate who had taught Septimus seamanship, passed it on to the junior midshipman. Mr Quinn went below to the midshipmen's berth.

Fitzroy Cocker and Charles Barry were sitting at the table, looking weary after their labours. Barry was writing in his private log, and Cocker, who had not managed to board the French ship until the brief fighting was over, was sitting with a glass of wine in his hand staring sullenly into space.

'Well, gentlemen,' said Septimus in his usual grave manner, 'we are heading for the French coast again.'

'Very interesting, demme!' sneered Cocker. 'Maybe you'll get another chance of skulking in the bushes and letting others do the dirty work, young lickspittle, eh?'

Septimus ignored him. 'The gunner's mate, Mr Preece, has

been ordered to take charge of a water party,' he continued. 'Boats are to land on a deserted part of the coast to take in water. Mr Barry will be with that landing-party, and I have asked Mr Gifford to allow Mr Cocker and myself to go also.'

'Oh, have you!' snarled Cocker, sitting up angrily. 'I'll take no favours from you, young—'

'I think you will take this one,' said Septimus gently, and bending forward he struck the senior midshipman hard on the cheek.

Barry exclaimed and started to his feet. Cocker, with a hand to his smitten cheek, stared with bulging eyes, unable to speak for wrath.

'You insulted me this afternoon, Mr Cocker,' continued Midshipman Quinn steadily, 'and you have just repeated the insult. I don't expect an apology from a bully of your kind. You have taken a blow from me, and I now wait to see whether you are the gentleman you boast yourself to be.'

Fitzroy Cocker's red face had gone white. He stood up very stiffly, all the bluster gone out of him.

'You'll fight, of course,' he said between his teeth.

'Of course,' nodded Septimus coolly.

Barry stepped forward hastily. 'Now see here, Quinn and Cocker, this thing mustn't be allowed to—'

'Pistol, Mr Quinn,' said Cocker as if Barry had not spoken. 'I name Mr Barry as my second, if he will act for me.'

With that, he turned on his heel and went out of the cabin.

2

In the greying light of dawn the *Althea* crept like a ghost ship towards the enemy shore. She was already close in, for Captain Sainsbury had come as near as he dared in darkness to reduce the chances of anyone ashore seeing her. Not that there was much chance of that, because this part of the coast was practically a desert. It was the low sandy coastline west of the Mouths of the Rhône, a place of endless tall sandhills with marshy lagoons behind them inland, the nearest towns or villages being eight or ten miles from the coast.

In the chains the leadsmen were chanting as they swung the lead-lines to measure the depth of water.

'By the mark seven . . . and a half eight . . . quarter less eight . . . by the mark seven . . .'

'Let go!'

The anchor cable's roar as it raced out through the hawse hole followed the captain's order. The topsails under which the frigate had been sailing were furled, she checked to the pull of her anchor, and lay motionless under the paling sky a quarter of a mile offshore.

The choice of anchorage had been well made. A semi-circular bay, bounded by low sandhills, had as its centre a narrow glen where a stream of fresh water issued from the inland lagoons. To eastward of the bay a long arm of land stretched out protectingly to end in a reef of yellow rock. This basis of rock supported a ridge of sandhills high enough to conceal the *Althea*'s masts from anyone approaching from the east. Westward the flat shores curved away to the horizon with no sign of life or human dwellings.

No time was lost in getting the boats away. It was still an hour before sunrise when the men of the water-party pulled ashore with the repaired water-casks and landed on the sand of the bay. Septimus, as he splashed through the shallows and reached the shadowy beach, was feeling a little nervous. This was the second time he had set foot on enemy territory, and it was quite possible that he would not leave it again.

Further along the beach Fitzroy Cocker and Charles Barry were landing from another boat. Cocker and Septimus had treated each other with the utmost politeness since the challenge, as two duellists were bound to do before the 'affair'. Mr Preece, the gunner's mate, had been let into the secret, for Septimus had to have a second and Preece could be trusted. The old Welshman had shaken his grizzled head when Midshipman Quinn had approached him with his request.

'I don't like it, Mr Quinn, sir,' he had said. 'No, indeed. I tell you now, asking your pardon, it's tamn foolishness. But I see well the matter must be settled somehow, so I'll act for you, sir – though I will be praying no one is hurt, yess, indeed!'

At this moment Mr Preece was giving instructions to Roberts the carpenter as to the filling of the casks.

'Mr Cocker and Mr Barry, with Mr Quinn and myself,' he finished, 'will be going over them sandhills to keep a watch. Look to it that you waste no time, now, Roberts!'

The seamen were getting the empty casks ashore while others went along the stream looking for a suitable place for filling them. Cocker and Barry came along the beach. Barry, whose face wore a worried expression, was carrying a long case under his arm.

'Where do you suggest, Mr Preece?' he asked, trying to appear as calm as a duellist's second should be.

The gunner's mate pointed to the sandhills. 'Beyond the crest, sir, if that's your pleasure.'

'It isn't my pleasure at all, but we must be out of sight of the ship and the water-party. That'll do.'

The four started to walk up the beach, Septimus and Mr Preece leading. The soft sand of the steep dunes had to be climbed, and some of the grave dignity of the procession was lost in the stumbling and tumbling. Barry lost his footing and went head over heels, and the expression on his face as he picked himself up again made Septimus want to laugh. This was not, he told himself severely, a proper state of mind for a person about to engage in a duel. When he discovered that Barry had twisted his ankle in the fall, he was less amused.

As they approached the crest of the sandhills Mr Preece muttered a warning in the ear of his 'principal'.

'Better come gradual-like over the skyline, Mr Quinn, sir. If so be as there's any Frenchies t'other side we'll have to find another spot.'

That, too, struck Septimus as funny. Here they were, sneaking about on enemy territory looking for a quiet place where two of them could kill each other, when there might be armed men waiting for them who would shoot all four of them out of hand. That was unlikely, however, for this huge area of lagoon and marsh was a bad place for a British landing and would therefore not be patrolled or guarded. Certainly there was no one to see the four heads that poked themselves cautiously over the dune-crest to peer through the course marram-grass that grew there. The sight that met their gaze was unexpected.

On their left lower sandhills undulated away to where broad lagoons and marshes stretched level into the morning haze. On their right tall dunes hid the countryside. But straight in front of them, running towards the northern distance, was a broad strip of grassy ground broken here and there by rocks – evidently the rock reef east of the bay was the end of a solid peninsula of rock rising from the marshes. This was not all. A mile or more away on the grassy flat were clumps of stunted trees and the shapes of low buildings, and a track leading from them and disappearing behind the dunes on their right showed that men or animals came that way.

'This won't do, gentlemen,' said Preece in a low voice. 'By your leave, I suggest we abandon our plan.'

'I agree,' Barry said with relief in his tone.

Cocker snorted. 'Well, I don't. We've come here to fight and we've not time to waste. The water-party will be ready in half an hour. Perhaps Mr Quinn also thinks of abandoning the plan?'

The sneer irritated Septimus, who would otherwise have been inclined to side with the others.

'Mr Cocker is right,' he declared. 'This opportunity of settling our difference must be taken. There's no one about and those buildings are probably a farm. There's a flat space further down that suits our purpose.'

'Aye aye, sir,' sighed Mr Preece. 'Then I'll suggest we goes well down on this side, so as to be more out of view from them buildings.'

They slid and stumbled down from the crest, through a lower rank of dunes, and over a third barrier before they reached a secluded little plateau between two sandhills and overlooking the green flat fifty feet below.

'Good enough,' Barry said, with a nervous glance at Preece. 'Shall we – begin?'

Everyone now became exceedingly formal. Septimus and Cocker retired to each end of the little plateau while Barry and Mr Preece conferred together in the middle. It was rapidly growing lighter now, and Septimus noticed the colours developing in his surroundings. The sand glowed pinkish-brown, the flat lands stretching away inland showed emerald green for the marshy ground and steel-blue where the lagoons spread their shallow waters. Far beyond the long strip of solid land the shapes of distant hills stood against the sky. And he noticed now that those low buildings had a mast beside them, with a flag of some kind hanging from it.

Mr Preece came towards him. His wrinkled face was solemn.

'Thirty paces, sir, if you're content. Mr Barry says I'm to ask if you won't agree to call off this duel, supposing Mr Cocker thinks the same way.'

'He won't,' replied Septimus. 'But you'll please to say that if Mr Cocker will apologise for his past conduct and mend his ways in future, I am willing to call it off.'

The gunner's mate hurried away with this message, and quickly returned to report that Cocker would certainly not apologise. He then went back to Barry, who had opened the case of pistols. Together the two seconds tested the flints and loaded with powder and ball. Together – looking, Septimus thought, extremely absurd – they measured out the thirty paces. Once more Mr Preece returned to his principal, this time to place him in position with his back turned towards Cocker, who was being similarly placed by Charles Barry.

'Mr Quinn, sir,' said Preece, 'here's your pistol. You're to stand as you are until the word *Fire*! is given. Mr Barry will—'

He stopped speaking suddenly, his grey head cocked to one side.

'Tamn!' he muttered. 'My old ears is playing tricks, indeed. You didn't hear a bugle-call, sir, now?'

'No,' replied Septimus.

The feel of the cold pistol-butt in his hand had made him

realise that in a few seconds he was to be the target for Fitzroy Cocker's bullet. He had to fight down the paralysing fear that crept up his spine. It was his own doing, after all, and if he escaped alive after standing Cocker's fire the senior midshipman would never again be able to insult him – in fact, Cocker would be made to feel ashamed. For Septimus intended to discharge his own weapon into the air after allowing Cocker to fire at him.

'Mr Barry will give the word, sir,' Preece was saying. 'He'll give *One-Two-Three-Fire*, and on that you'll turn and pull trigger. You can cock your pistol now. Are you ready, sir?'

'Yes,' said Septimus steadily.

'And heaven forgive me for aiding and abetting such tamn foolishness, yess indeed!' muttered Mr Preece as he hurried away.

Septimus stood with the pistol in his lowered hand, staring in front of him. His position was at the eastward end of the duelling ground, and he could see the place where the ridge of the higher sandhills came down to meet the flat green stretch. The green flat passed behind the ridge as if quite a big area was hidden there. In the fast-increasing light of morning it looked a pleasant place to wander and explore, though not so pleasant as the far-off fields and copses round Linton Abbott. It would be nearing harvest-time in Hampshire now, and the thought of leafy shades and quiet streams made him suddenly homesick.

'One!'

Charles's voice sounded quite shaky. It must be an unpleasant business being a second in a duel.

'Two!'

Immediately after that word had been uttered, Septimus heard what sounded like an echo of it, coming from some distance away – perhaps from that ridge of sandhill. His gaze sharpened as he stared down at the spot where green flat and brown sandhill met.

'Three!'

'Stop!'

The voice of Midshipman Quinn prevented the speaking of the fatal command to fire. Cocker swung round angrily, Mr Preece and Barry stared in astonishment. They saw Septimus crouching on all fours and gesturing urgently to them to do the same.

'What in the name of Hades,' began Cocker wrathfully, and was stopped by Barry's hand gripping his shoulder.

'Quiet – and get down!' said Charles, in a hoarse whisper.

Mr Preece was already crawling towards Septimus. The three of them crept to the edge of their plateau and lay flat on their stomachs beside Septimus to peer downward through the thin stems of the marram-grass. They saw at once why Mr Quinn had committed the unusual crime of calling off a duel at the last moment.

Marching rather raggedly round the corner of the sandhill came a small column of armed men. They had bits and pieces of uniform – here and there a military shako and a cross-belt or two – but nearly every man carried a musket on his shoulder. The officer who marched beside them wore the blue uniform of the French infantry. The column was only two hundred yards from where the four lay, and about fifty feet below the level of their sandy plateau.

'Well now, bless me!' muttered Mr Preece. 'What will they be doing here, at this hour of the morning?'

'D'you think they've seen us?' Barry asked.

'Not they, sir. I reckon they're like our militia – volunteers in training. Look now, the officer's halted 'em to start drilling.'

Septimus looked at Cocker. 'My apologies for interrupting our affair, Mr Cocker,' he whispered. 'As you see, a pistol-shot would have endangered all four of us.'

'You're right,' Cocker grunted. 'And I tell you what – we'd better not waste a second. If those fellows happen to get on the crest of the dunes, they'll see the water-party – and shoot 'em down like dogs. Come on!'

He started to wriggle back and get to his feet. Next moment Septimus, who had done the same, grabbed him and pulled him back.

'Too late!' he said coolly. 'We seem to have got into the middle of our French friends' field-day. Look up there!'

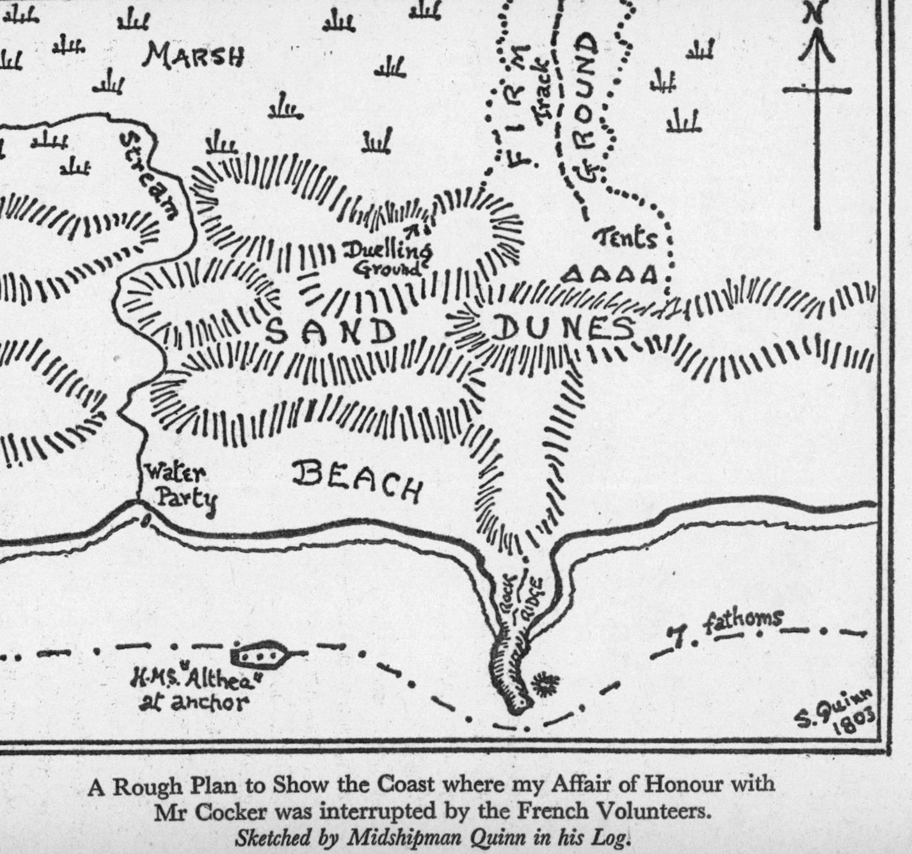

A Rough Plan to Show the Coast where my Affair of Honour with Mr Cocker was interrupted by the French Volunteers.
Sketched by Midshipman Quinn in his Log.

The others followed the direction of his pointing finger. Moving along the flank of the sandhills above them was another line of armed men. They were cut off from the beach.

3

Luckily the spot where the duelling party were crouching was a fairly good hiding place. The little plateau was a sort of narrow shelf on the lower face of the sand dunes, just above where they fell to merge in the flat land behind them. It was narrow at the end, and partly overhung by the sandhill above it, which gave cover from anyone looking down from the crest above. By lying flat on this sandy ledge, they could also escape observation by anyone passing below. The column of men at the foot of the dunes was so close that the words of the officer in command sounded quite loud. Charles Barry, after listening for a minute, turned a worried face to his companions.

'I think they know we're here!' he announced in a whisper. 'The officer's just told his men that they will advance up the sandhills in five minutes' time, to attack the enemy.'

'They would close in without waiting to announce it, if that was the case,' Septimus pointed out. 'No, Charles. I think this is a force of volunteers practising army manœuvres. The enemy is that line of men up above us, and they'll be defending a position.'

'That's it!' exclaimed Mr Preece. 'And I'll wager my whiskers, gentlemen, that the defending force will fall back and take another position on the crest – I've seen our lads doing the same at Shoreham Camp, yess indeed!'

Cocker put his red head into the conference. His blue eyes were gleaming.

'Then we'll have to fight for our lives,' he said hoarsely. 'We're between the two forces and they're bound to see us when they start closing in.'

'There must be forty or fifty of them,' whispered Barry, 'and nearly all have muskets – we haven't a chance, with only two loaded pistols between four of us.'

'Worse than that,' Septimus added. 'If they withdraw to the crest as Mr Preece thinks they will, the men on the beach are doomed. Our duty is to them, gentlemen. They must be warned.'

Below them the file of French volunteers was being formed for the mock attack. There was not a moment to lose if the seamen on the beach were to be saved from the deadly fire which would be poured in upon them if the French reached the crest and caught them unawares.

'Here's my plan,' said Septimus rapidly – he had that moment thought of it. 'One of us must show himself and draw the enemy's attention. He must make the whole force pursue him westward if he can. The rest must get over the crest as soon as the way's clear and order the water-party to embark and pull back to the frigate. It's the only way—'

'I'll stay and draw them,' Barry interrupted.

'You've damaged your ankle. The man who stays must be able to run. I shall be that man.'

Septimus's words brought so vehement a protest from the others that he thought for a moment that the French would hear and discover them.

'No time for argument!' he cut them short. 'It's my plan and I carry it out.'

'Not alone,' rapped Fitzroy Cocker. 'I'm coming with you. Mr Barry, Mr Preece, you'll get back to the beach as soon as possible. Do as Mr Quinn advises.'

'The French are starting up the dunes!' Barry announced.

'Come on, then, Cocker.'

Septimus started to creep away along the sand shelf. Mr Preece's anxious voice made him halt.

'Mr Quinn, sir, where will you head for?'

'The rocky headland – if we get through. Good luck!'

A moment later he and Cocker were crouching side by side at the other end of the shelf, pistol in hand. Below on their right the line of Frenchmen was advancing up the slope, but they were still hidden from the men on the dunes above.

'Ready?'

'Aye – ready!'

Both midshipmen leaped together on to the top of a sandy hillock. For a second or two they stood there, conspicuous figures in their white knee-breeches and blue coats. Cocker took off his hat and waved it aloft. His red hair was a splash of brilliant colour in the light, for in a very short time now the sun would rise.

They were seen. A shout from the 'defenders' of the sand-hills was caught up and repeated by the men advancing from below.

'*Voilà – Anglais? Oui, Anglais!*'

The yell of '*Anglais!*' echoed among the sandhills as fifty throats took up the cry. Septimus saw the line of men coming diagonally down the dunes towards them, brandishing their muskets. As he gripped Cocker's elbow and thrust him forward he caught sight of a blue shako rising above a crest of sand not twenty yards down the hill. They had nearly waited too long.

'You lead!' he shouted to Cocker.

They ran for it like a pair of rabbits, dodging among the dips and crests of the sandhills. And after them, yelling themselves hoarse, pounded the fifty volunteers intent on capturing the first representatives of the hated English nation they had ever seen. Septimus hoped sincerely that no one among them had the sense to realise that the presence of two English naval officers meant that they had landed somewhere nearby with other Englishmen. He also realised that if some genius among the pursuit had a loaded musket and stopped to take aim and fire, he might bring down one of the fugitives. For although Cocker was taking an excellent line that afforded all possible cover, the two were in view for most of the way – and the leading Frenchmen were no more than fifty paces behind them.

Cocker's longer legs were holding a fast pace. Septimus was hard put to it to keep on his heels. But the plan was succeeding. They had drawn the whole party away from Barry and Preece, who must by now be on their way to warn the seamen on the beach.

Crash!

The report, and the loud buzzing of something flying above his head, told that one man at least had thought of firing his musket. If that was to be repeated many times either he or Cocker was bound to be hit. And they had to find a way of doubling on their tracks, too, for at present they were running westward, away from the rocky headland where – if they were lucky – they might be taken off by one of the frigate's boats.

Within another half-minute the opportunity presented itself. The sloping dune beneath their feet seemed to break off in a small precipice, and he saw a little below them the glitter of a stream. This must be the stream from which the *Althea*'s men were filling their casks on the other side of the sandhills. It had carved a deep and narrow course, a miniature canyon, in its passage, and the water sped along in a bed four feet deep, bordered here and there by scrubby thorn-bushes.

'Stream-bed – hide!' he managed to gasp as he and Cocker half-ran, half-fell down the slope into the glen.

Cocker understood. With hardly a second to spare before the pursuers would appear on the edge above, both midshipmen sprang down into the stream. It was only a couple of feet in depth and the water was far from cold. In a moment they were lying pressed against the sandy bank, which overhung slightly, where a fringe of bushes grew close to the edge. With most of their bodies under water and their faces against the sand, they supported themselves with the hands that grasped their pistols. The bushes concealed that one sign of their presence.

It was an uncomfortable position to adopt but they would not have to hold it for long. Down the wall of sand the pursuers came sliding and shouting, to gallop to the stream and leap across it. Some of them jumped short and fell in, and one Frenchman took off from very close to the bushes which sheltered Septimus – so close that the sand he kicked into the water splashed the midshipman's face.

This was the danger period. Anyone looking back from the further side of the stream might easily see the two dark-blue arms clutching the bank. But the volunteers were too excited to consider a backward glance, though someone could be heard breathlessly demanding whether he should go down the river-course and try to cut off the *sacrés Anglais*. A man with a loud voice told him to come on and stop being a fool. Which, Septimus reflected, was just as well, for the man might have emerged on the beach and seen the water-party. By this time the *Althea*'s men should have received the warning, and – with Barry and Preece – would be hastily embarking their casks to pull back to the frigate.

The noise of pursuit died away. The two midshipmen had scrambled dripping out of their hiding-place the moment the last Frenchman had vanished into the dunes, for it could not be long before the enemy realised that there was no one in front of them. It was tempting to think that a brisk trot down the stream-bed would bring them to the beach and the possibility of safety, but that they dared not do. Fifty men with muskets could wreak havoc among sixteen seamen armed with cutlasses. They dashed upstream, Cocker leading, and round the inland base of the sandhills.

Even as they turned eastward on level ground, a chorus of distant angry shouts told them that their ruse had been discovered.

'We've got a good lead,' panted Cocker over his shoulder. 'They'll not catch us now.'

Septimus had not breath enough to answer, but he hoped Cocker was right. He himself was getting near the end of his strength. He wondered whether to throw away the heavy pistol he still carried, but decided to keep it. There might be use for it yet.

Fresh yells from the rear broke out. They had been seen. Two muskets crashed, but no bullets came near them. Cocker increased his pace and Septimus, with a great effort, managed to keep up. The senior midshipman was making for the foot of the ridge of dune close to their former hiding-place. Once round the corner of that ridge they could head seaward, following the crest until they reached the tip of the rocky peninsula. Again a musket banged and the shot went wide. Round the corner they raced – to halt in dismay.

In front of them was a grassy plain under the dunes, and across it stood a line of tents. Plainly this was the camp of the French recruits. Three men were standing together near the tents, talking and gesticulating – probably they were discussing the musket-shots they had heard.

'Come on – at 'em!' shouted Cocker, and dashed forward.

Septimus, gripping his pistol, followed. The Frenchmen sprang round at Cocker's shout. Two of them had muskets in their hands, but only one of them managed to raise his weapon before the red-haired midshipman was upon them. Cocker's fist smashed into the man's chin as he dashed the levelled musket aside with his other arm. Septimus, a few yards behind, saw the third man sweep up his sword for a downward cut at Cocker, and fired his pistol at point-blank range. The swordsman fell, but the remaining Frenchman, swinging his musket by the barrel, aimed a tremendous blow at Septimus, who ducked under it and fell flat. Then Cocker's pistol exploded deafeningly close to his ear and Cocker's hand dragged him to his feet.

'On! On!' yelled the senior midshipman exultingly.

The three camp guards appeared to be the only men in the camp. Flinging their useless pistols away, the two dashed up the sandhill behind the tents and reached the crest almost exhausted. In front of them the dunes dipped in a long ridge to seaward, and at the end of the ridge, jutting into a sea glittering in the first rays of the rising sun, was the rocky point which might mean safety.

There lay the *Althea*, too – sails were appearing on her yards as she prepared to get under way. And there, just pulling out from her side to head for the rocky point, was a boat. A glance behind them showed the van of the pursuit streaming round the corner, too far behind now to catch them.

'We've done it, Sep!' gasped Cocker, turning to grin triumphantly at his companion.

'Not quite,' returned Septimus quietly, and pointed down the sandy hill they had just climbed.

A man was mounting rapidly, not a hundred feet below them. And he carried a musket. It was the man Cocker had hit. He saw them, but did not offer to shoot. He had seen their empty pistols and was going to close on them before firing – he was going to make sure. Unarmed, they would have no chance. They turned with one accord and ran on, up and down the undulations of the sandy ridge.

Septimus threw a glance over his shoulder as they approached the rockier part of the ridge. The pursuer, who had not had to chase over dunes for fifteen minutes, was gaining on them fast. He was fifty paces behind. The *Althea*'s boat was still a long way from the point, but the narrowing ridge had sea on both sides now.

They raced on desperately, with loose stones underfoot. Septimus felt he must collapse with bursting lungs at any moment. And then came the loud report of the musket, very close behind him. He heard the bullet sing past – the shot had missed. As he realised this he saw Cocker, a few feet ahead of him, stumble and fall. The bullet had hit him in the left thigh.

'Run, you fool – leave me!' groaned the red-headed boy as Septimus bent over him. 'I'm done.'

Septimus straightened himself and looked back. Twenty paces away the Frenchman had halted to reload his musket. As he rammed in the charge he looked full at Septimus, grinning savagely.

While the midshipman hesitated a shout floated across the water – 'Jump, sir – jump!' It came from the swiftly-approaching boat. He saw that he could plunge from his present position into the water, thence to be picked up and taken to safety. But his decision was already made.

Stooping, he picked up a large and rugged stone. The Frenchman's musket was levelled when Septimus made his desperate rush, but the stone was hurtling through the air as he pulled the trigger. The midshipman felt the sting of powder-grains on his cheek a second before he hurled his small body at the man.

Half-stunned by the impact of the stone on the side of his head, the man went down before that furious charge. Septimus, gasping for breath, picked himself up and saw that his enemy was lying still. His head had struck against a sharp rock in his fall. Septimus picked up the musket and slung it over the side of the ridge before going to help the wounded Cocker down to the boat and safety.

4

In the afternoon of the day of the water-party, Lieutenant Gifford came down the companionway into the midshipmen's berth with Midshipman Quinn at his heels. Both had been on duty on the quarterdeck until then. They found Fitzroy Cocker sitting somewhat awkwardly on a chair padded with blankets, his bandaged leg stretched out in front of him, talking to Charles Barry.

'At ease, Mr Barry,' nodded the lieutenant pleasantly as Barry sprang to his feet. 'I've looked in to see how our invalid is progressing.'

'With respect, sir,' said Mr Cocker, grinning, 'I'm as fit as you are. Demme, what's a flesh-wound in the thigh?'

'A mere nothing, I'm sure, to a Cocker,' smiled Mr Gifford. 'You realise, of course,' he added, 'that but for Mr Quinn here you might have had something more than a flesh wound.'

Fitzroy Cocker looked up with a frown. 'Naturally I realise it, sir. And I'm glad you're here to listen to what I'm about to say to him.' He turned to Septimus. 'Mr Quinn, I apologise unreservedly for the insult I offered you, and for otherwise behaving like a – well, as I did behave, demme! You saved my life—'

'You saved mine, remember,' put in the junior midshipman.

'Don't stop me talking, demme! I've more to say. If you would – I mean, if I – that's to say, I'd value your friendship—'

His gruff voice ceased. Septimus was holding out his hand.

'Pray don't distress yourself, Mr Cocker,' he said in his dignified way. 'You have it.'

Chapter Five

The Knight-Errant

I

'Sail-ho!'

The lookout's cry from the crows'-nest produced a bustle of excitement on board His Majesty's frigate *Althea.* For three weeks she had been cruising on an enemy coast, and each time that cry had sounded there had been an enemy vessel on the horizon. Captain Sainsbury showed no anxiety to send his crew to their action-stations, however. For once, the chances were against that distant sail being a French one.

For some time now the British raider's presence in the North Mediterranean had been known to the French. Her last action – a night landing to burn the shipping in Olonville Harbour – had been so successful that Captain Sainsbury, considering that the enemy might well risk sending out a squadron to sink or capture so impudent a ship, had decided to withdraw to southward for a few days until things had quietened down. This withdrawal had taken him into a latitude where it was very rare for a French vessel to venture, for Nelson was at Toulon and British warships were continually passing between the British Admiral and Gibraltar. Captain Sainsbury believed the strange sail was much more likely to be a British ship than a Frenchman.

And so it proved. Half-an-hour later the frigate had spoken to the *Imperious* sloop-of-war, carrying despatches and mails from Toulon. It was a fortunate encounter, for the *Imperious* had on board a considerable packet of mail for the *Althea,* whose destination at the end of her mission was Toulon.

There was much rejoicing on board that day. In the midshipmen's berth Charles Barry and Septimus Quinn, who had the watch-below, sat reading their letters. There were several for Barry, but Septimus, who had no relatives except his uncle, had to be content with a long and beautifully-written sermon from the Reverend Theophilus Quinn. Even that made pleasant reading, however, reminding him of the cool shade of trees on the Rectory lawn, and bringing the scent of English summer flowers to his nostrils instead of the mingled odours of tar, bilge-water and tallow candles which was the smell of the stuffy cabin.

'I say!' exclaimed Charles suddenly. He looked up from the letter he was reading. 'This is from Philippa – my sister, you know, who was in the Portsmouth coach when the highwaymen stopped it. I'd no idea you foiled the toby-man single-handed, my lad!'

'I assure you I did not, Charles,' replied Septimus.

'Well, Philippa says you did. She relates the whole story here and seemes to regard you as a genuine hero. Girls are like that – romantic.'

He resumed his reading, and Septimus, who had gone rather red, adjusted his spectacles and concentrated his attention on the excellent advice of the Reverend Theophilus. After a moment's silence Barry burst into sudden laughter.

'Listen to this,' he said, waving his sister's letter. 'When I parted from Philippa I told her – jokingly, you know – that I'd fight the French as her knight-errant and send her an account of my victories. This is what she writes. 'A real knight-errant would send me something more than letters – a Frenchman's moustache, for instance".' He broke off to laugh again. 'Be thankful you haven't any sisters, Sep. A Frenchman's moustache! What next?'

'Are you going to get one for her?' inquired Midshipman Quinn.

Barry glanced sharply at him, but the spectacled midshipman appeared to be serious.

'Oh, I'll send her the coloured pebble I picked up last time we landed on French soil,' he said carelessly. 'I daresay that'll please her. Hullo, Fitz! What's new on deck?'

Midshipman Fitzroy Cocker came down the companionway, ducking his red head under the deck-beams, and flung himself down beside them.

'We're still heading east of north,' he said, 'and there's a spanking westerly breeze carrying us towards Boney's Empire again.'

'That's not news – we've been on that course since we spoke to *Imperious*,' retorted Charles. 'Isn't there any buzz about our next raid?'

'Well, demme! There's a rumour, if you can call it news,' Cocker replied. 'Preece swears he had it from the Third Officer—'

'Mr Preece was right last time about our destination,' put in Septimus.

'So he was, Sep. Well, I hope he's right again, because' – Cocker's blue eyes sparkled – 'there'll be a rare scrap if he is. You remember the French engineer we captured during the Olonville raid, and the yarn he spun?'

'About the giant gun and the new fort?' nodded Barry. 'Yes – a very tall story, I thought. Might have been one of yours.'

Cocker threw his hat at him. 'It's been confirmed, it seems,' he said. 'The *Imperious* confirmed it. A spy brought the story to Gibraltar and the captain of the *Imperious* was told about it by the port admiral. The French have pretty well completed a new fort on the point five miles south of Marseilles – Fort Flambeau they call it – and they've got the gun there.'

'What! Not this monster cannon?'

'So they say, or so the spy says. It can hurl a ball twice as far as our guns, according to report. The name they've got for it is Jean le Terrible.'

'Terrible Jack, eh?' grinned Barry. 'But come to the rumour, Fitz. How does the *Althea* come in?'

'Demme, how d'you think? We're going to have a look at Fort Flambeau, and I'll wager my head Captain Sainsbury will do more than look at it. Maybe we'll dodge the shots from Terrible Jack and go in to bombard the fort.'

Septimus removed his spectacles and wiped them thoughtfully.

'I hardly think he will do that,' he remarked.

A week ago Fitzroy Cocker would have told him to hold his tongue or given him a cuff on the ear. Like Charles Barry, however, he had come to respect Midshipman Quinn's sayings and doings, having learned that both were always to the point.

'What's your idea, Sep?' he asked.

'It depends on the lie of the land,' said the junior midshipman slowly, 'but as a provisional scheme I would land a party to attack the fort in rear, if that were possible. You see, gentlemen, this fort has clearly been built to resist attack from the sea. With this huge gun far out-ranging any ship's guns, it would be folly to close the fort from seaward – except by way of a feint attack.'

'There's something in that, demme!' agreed Cocker. 'Though mark you,' he added, 'I don't like the idea of creeping on the Frogs from behind. Fight 'em face to face, say I!'

'Pray allow me to disagree, Fitz,' Septimus protested. 'A surprise attack is perfectly fair in war.'

'Hear, hear!' came from Barry.

'I maintain,' continued Septimus earnestly, 'that any weapon or form of attack is fair against the French, For instance, if they invent a gun called Terrible Jack, which can throw a cannon-ball twice as far as our largest ship cannon, why should we not answer them by inventing some other sort of weapon? This war isn't a game. It's a life-and-death struggle between Napoleon and the only nation who is left to stand against him. It's merely reasonable—'

'All right, all right – I surrender!' broke in Cocker, waving his hands. 'I grant you it's reasonable, Sep, but you reduce war to the level of a business. You'd never make a knight-errant, demme!'

'I suppose I wouldn't,' responded Mr Midshipman Quinn, looking suddenly very thoughtful.

Further debate was cut short by the arrival of a messenger requesting Midshipmen Barry and Cocker to report on the quarterdeck with their sextants. Septimus, whose rapid proficiency in navigation caused him to be excused from this exercise, took a home-made apron from a hook on the cabin bulkhead and went to look for Mr Preece, the Welsh gunner's mate, with whom he had business. As he went he continued to ponder Fitzroy Cocker's last remark.

The sound of the frigate's many voices increased with every foot of his descent, for he was going into the very bowels of the ship. The timbers and crossbeams creaked with the slight roll, the planking groaned as she curtseyed on the waves, the thousand-and-one articles that hung or were secured in various places about the huge framework of wood that was the *Althea* added their small tappings or scrapings to swell the noise. Down in the narrowed bottom of the frigate these noises became less again. Here was the cable-locker where the great ropes were coiled like sleeping snakes, the paint locker, and the carpenter's store. Mr Preece had commandeered a corner here for his workshop, being of a handy turn with tools. The place had just about enough elbow-room for one man to use a plane, and when two persons were in it, it was overcrowded. However, Septimus was small for his fifteen years and Mr Preece, who was sixty, was not a large man, so they were able to work side by side.

As Septimus had expected, the old Welshman was spending part of his watch-below in his 'cubby', as he called it.

'Come you in here, now, Mr Quinn,' was his greeting. 'I'm working on that casing we were talking about, for Little Jim.'

Septimus, edging his way into the narrow space where a small oil-lamp burned in a safety container devised by Mr Preece, knew that 'Little Jim' was the Welshman's nickname for a certain experiment on which they were engaged. No one else – not even Charles Barry – had been told about Little Jim. It was an idea that had come to Midshipman Quinn during the starlit hours of an uneventful Middle Watch, and he had enlisted Mr Preece to help him put it into material form.

'Very thin, that iron casing is, yess indeed,' continued Mr Preece, holding up a round shell slightly larger than a cricketball. 'Here's the hole for the slow-match, see.'

'Where did you get this?' asked Septimus, taking the shell to examine it.

'Tod Beamish made it for me, sir. He's taken Phillips's berth.'

Phillips, the ship's blacksmith, had been killed in the last encounter with an enemy ship.

'He asked no questions, and he won't split on us,' added the gunner's mate with schoolboyish glee. 'Will it do, Mr Quinn, sir?'

'It will do very well. It should stand the force of the expanding gases. We must have about eight very small holes drilled in this, Mr Preece, distributed all over the surface. And we must have four of them.'

Mr Preece nodded his grey head, and then pointed to some bottles and packages that stood in a rack above his narrow bench.

'Is there enough fillings for four little Jims, now, sir?'

'Just about. Pray tell me, Mr Preece – do you think we shall attack Fort Flambeau?'

'I do reckon so, sir. This gun – Terrible Jack – will be a proper danger to our shipping if any comes within range, d'ye see, and Captain Sainsbury, he's not the man to sail past without a try. Our course is set for Fort Flambeau at this very moment, yess indeed.'

Midshipman Quinn, who had put on his spectacles to examine the casing, took them off again and frowned at them. There was the light of a scheme in his eye.

'If Captain Sainsbury adopts the plan I think he'll adopt,' he said, 'he'll need every man of the *Althea*'s complement – including myself, you, and Beamish. How long before we're off Point Flambeau, Mr Preece?'

'If this wind holds, sir, you might say thirty-six hours.'

'Can Beamish make three more of these shells within twenty-four hours?'

'I do reckon so, sir. Why so, if I may be so bold?'

'Because I've a mind to try what Little Jim can do against Terrible Jack,' said Mr Quinn, and left Mr Preece in his cubby scratching his head.

It was less than twenty-four hours later when the captain of the *Althea* summoned all his officers and midshipmen to the main cabin. The frigate was lying hove-to seven miles from the French coast, or that part of it – just south of the big port of Marseilles –

where Point Flambeau jutted far out into the Mediterranean. Captain Sainsbury had had an enlarged copy of a section of the chart made and hung on the bulkhead of the cabin.* He spoke for ten minutes in his calm, rather hard voice, and no speaker ever had a more attentive audience, for he was outlining the proposed attack on Fort Flambeau. Then he rose from his chair and went to stand by the big plan.

'Stand round, gentlemen,' he said, 'and take note of every detail. In less than sixteen hours you will all, with the exception of Mr Haswell, be ashore on the enemy territory represented on this plan. At least, I hope so. Your landing depends on whether the outlet of this stream, which you see coming down to a cove a quarter-of-a-mile north-east of the fort, affords a landing-place.' He pointed to a curving line running down from northward to the coast. 'You will observe that elsewhere the coast round Point Flambeau consists of steep cliffs. The fort itself is hexagonal in shape, and – judging by the road to it which is marked here – has its entry port on the north side. That road passes through a defile between two small hills about three hundred yards north of the fort. The eastern hill is a ridge which rises close above the stream. Is that clear to all of you?'

He waited until each of his listeners had answered. Lieutenant Pyke, Lieutenant Gifford, Captain Salter of the Marines, and after them Midshipmen Cocker, Barry and Quinn, all replied that it was clear.

'Very well,' said the captain. 'Here is the plan. The *Althea*, with a skeleton crew and myself in command, Lieutenant Haswell assisting, will stand in for the point at first light. As I have said, the landing-parties will have rowed ashore during the night, and will have taken up positions. Captain Salter and his marines will be on the end of the eastern hill overlooking the road' – the Marine captain, a red-faced man with magnificent sidewhiskers, nodded – 'and Mr Pyke and Mr Gifford with their men will be concealed further to the east on the same ridge.'

* It was later copied into Midshipman Quinn's private log, from which the sketches and diagrams in this book are taken.

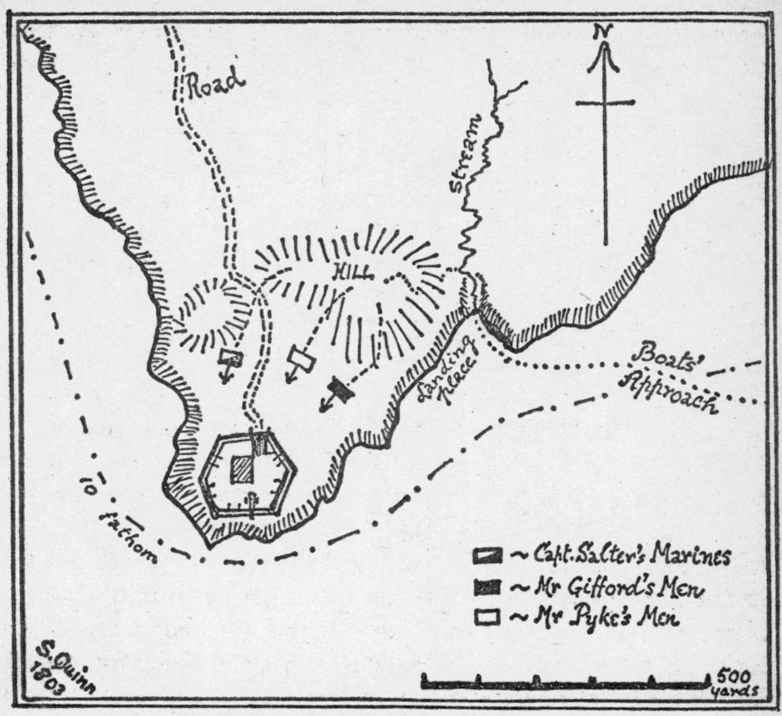

The French Fort Called Fort Flambeau, with a plan of the Successful Raid by H.M. Frigate *Althea.*
As drawn by Midshipman Quinn in his Log.

'The – er – the midshipmen, sir?' put in Fitzroy Cocker, greatly daring.'

'Thank you, Mr Cocker. I was about to give you your stations. You yourself will be with Mr Gifford's party. Mr Barry and Mr Quinn with Mr Pyke.'

Septimus repressed his disappointment. He liked Mr Gifford, while Lieutenant George Pyke was an old enemy of his.

'I expect to draw the fort's fire,' continued Captain Sainsbury. 'If this gun they call Jean le Terrible really exists, we shall give the French a little target practice with it. The first shot fired from the fort is your signal to attack. Captain Salter will leave one-third of his Marines to guard the defile in case of any enemy approach along the road, and attack west of the main gate. Mr Pyke will rush the main gate when the breach is made. Mr Gifford will attack the eastern walls. Your object will be to gain the walls unobserved, of course, while the French are busy with *Althea*.' He turned to the First Lieutenant. 'Mr Pyke, the general command of this expedition is yours. If you succeed in entering the fort, waste no time in rendering all guns useless – particularly this giant gun, if it exists. I suggest that Beamish – the strongest man on board – and the gunner's mate go with your party.'

'Aye aye, sir,' said Pyke.

'When your task is complete, withdraw as you came. Pull along the coast north-eastward for one mile, then head south-east to rejoin the ship. Has anyone a question to ask? No? Then that is all, gentlemen. I advise you to begin your preparations at once.'

No sooner were the three midshipmen out of the main cabin and on deck than Septimus made off for'ard.

'Hey!' cried Barry. 'Where are you bound for, Sep?'

'I am beginning my preparations, as the captain advised,' replied Midshipman Quinn. 'I want to warn Beamish that he'll have to carry something for me.'

2

Four boats crept silently in towards the dark uneven cliff-line of the French coast. The faint creak of oars was lost in the murmur of the sea against the rocks as they drew nearer and altered course a little to head for the inner corner of a small cove under the cliffs, where the four shapes merged in the black shadow. The September night was overcast and the sea was very slight – a perfect night for landing in enemy country.

A hoarse voice, pitched low, spoke as the first boat grated against the rock.

'All's well, sir – flat ledges here.'

'Quiet, confound you!' came Lieutenant Pyke's angry whisper.

There followed a confused clinking and trampling as the Marines landed first, their white cross-belts showing in the darkness and making them look like eerie skeletons. Orders were whispered, muskets slung. A seaman who had been sent to investigate the route came back to report that the stream-bed was all sharp rocks but could be followed. File by file, stealing from the boats like sea-ghosts come to invade the land, the *Althea*'s expeditionary force penetrated into Napoleon Bonaparte's territory once again.

Midshipman Septimus Quinn, clambering up the pitch-black gorge of the little stream and trying to keep his cutlass from banging against the rocks, spoke over his shoulder to Charles Barry.

'Charles! Has Beamish got that bag?'

'Yes,' came the whispered reply, 'he's just behind me with—'

A furious whisper – Mr Pyke's – interrupted him.

'Silence! Or by heaven, Mr Quinn, I'll send you back to the coast!'

It was perhaps reasonable to maintain a close silence, for although Fort Flambeau was a quarter of a mile away beyond low rugged hills a sound could carry far on such a still night. Septimus spoke no more.

The long file of men was climbing up the left-hand side of the miniature gorge now, and many were the smothered oaths as they came in contact with the spiny *maquis* bushes that grew in the cracks of the limestone. Once out of the gorge, it was plain that dawn was not far off. The low clouds were taking shape overhead and the outlines of rocks and bushes could be seen – which was just as well, for this was very rough ground. Lieutenant Pyke was leading the way, and leading well, as Septimus freely admitted. The thorns and rocks underfoot were on a steep slope, but this soon levelled out. They were on the crest of the eastern ridge of little hills.

With no more than a short whispered order the three parties separated. Mr Gifford's men dropped out of the file and were left to conceal themselves as best they could among the bushes and boulders. The Marines and Pyke's party went on for a short distance and then Pyke halted his forty men at the point where the ground began to drop again. The Marines went on down the slope to disappear in the shadows.

Septimus found himself a spot between two low thorn-bushes which seemed to grow on the edge of the downward slope, and lay down with his cutlass beside him to wait. A few yards away Barry was doing the same. From behind a large rock on his left came a cautious whisper.

'It's me here, sir – Beamish – and I've got the bag.'

All round them was the rustle and grunting of seamen finding themselves a comfortable lying position. Then silence, except for the muted twitter of small birds in the thickets – the sign that dawn was at hand.

Slowly the darkness paled and Mr Quinn's surroundings took shape. He saw first that there was a shallow valley or glen, only two or three hundred yards wide, at the foot of the slope in front of him. The flat-topped shape on its further side quickly revealed itself as Fort Flambeau. The light grew with astonishing speed, and soon he could see the upper half of a sentry moving on the wall of the fort. And he saw now why they had had to halt here instead of using the darkness to get closer to the fort – the ground between the hill and the walls of Fort Flambeau had been cleared of all cover, and the sentry could overlook every inch of it.

There was the sea beyond, even now showing a tint of blue. Fort Flambeau had been built on the very edge of the cliffs, with sea on two sides and on the east side only a narrow strip of rocky ground between the walls and the cliff-edge. That was where Mr Gifford and his men – and Fitzroy Cocker – would attack. Those new stone walls were at least twenty feet high, but the seamen had their own method of overcoming those. Mr Quinn felt in his side-pocket, where some tackle of his own reposed. The *Althea*'s sail-maker had been surprised when he was asked for the loan of his sharpest scissors. A faint and rather self-conscious smile spread over the junior midshipman's face as he fingered this strange weapon.

Below on his right he could see the pale thread of narrow road winding through the gap in the hills to the fort. On the hillside above it he caught a glint of red – those Marines were not well concealed. He hoped the sentry hadn't seen it. The massive gate of the fort looked formidable, but – again – the attackers had a plan for dealing with that. Septimus had watched Captain Salter superintending the manufacture of four small kegs during the previous afternoon. It crossed his mind that if those kegs failed to do their business thoroughly it would be a bad business for Mr Pyke's party.

He turned to whisper cautiously over his shoulder.

'Beamish!'

'Yessir?'

'Stick close to me until we're in the fort.'

'Aye aye, sir!'

Septimus returned his attention to the fort. In his other pocket was his small telescope. It was nearly light enough to use it now. He could see the flagstaff on the central buildings of the fort, and the flag hanging limply from it. That was like the Frogs – leaving their colours hoisted all night instead of lowering them at sunset and hoisting them at dawn, as was the British custom. Someone was stirring in that building, for a thin column of blue smoke was rising from it. The cook was starting to prepare breakfast, no doubt. The thought of that made Mr Quinn's mouth water, for he had eaten nothing since leaving the frigate four hours ago for the long pull shoreward. There was a piece of ship's biscuit – 'hard tack' – in his bulging pockets, and he nibbled at it to assuage the pangs of hunger.

That thin column of smoke was rising only a few feet, straight up in the air, before spreading out and vanishing in the morning haze. If the air was as still and heavy as that, Septimus meditated, there would be a good chance for Little Jim to show his effectiveness. But he hoped there was more breeze out at sea, or the *Althea* would be slow to appear over the horizon. He took out his telescope and scanned the grey-blue sea that stretched away to southward beyond the foreground of sloping hillside and cliff-edge. The horizon was just discernible through the haze, and he fancied he could see the three faint lines, very close together, that could be the frigate's masts. If she was hull-down now, she would soon be in view from the fort, if the sentry was wide awake enough to see her. Through the dim circle of the telescope he could see the head and shoulders of the sentry moving slowly round the walls, and could even make out his movements as he yawned. Poor Frog! He had probably been out on duty for four hours and was looking forward to some food and a doss-down in a warm bunk. Before long he would realise that he wasn't going to get them.

It was a tedious business, this waiting. In the bushes around him the seamen were beginning to get restless, as their movements and mutterings testified. Lieutenant Pyke's growl, threatening flogging to any man who made a sound, was heard more than once before the Fort Flambeau operation began.

It began with a bugle-call in the fort, sounding oddly loud on the calm air. At once Mr Quinn's telescope was trained on the walls, and since it was now almost full daylight he could see very well what was happening. The sentry had evidently seen the approaching frigate and given the alarm. Soldiers were appearing on the walls, blue-coated men running in disorderly fashion but sorting themselves into ranks. One group of about ten men formed close to the south rampart of the fort, where Septimus had noticed a long grey object like a massive rounded stone. He saw now, in the clearer light, that it was an enormous gun. That must be the famous Terrible Jack, and the ten men were Terrible Jack's gun-crew.

He swung his small telescope towards the sea. There was the *Althea*, still far out on the blue but a most beautiful sight, for she was under full sail and the white canvas was flushed pink with the reflected colour of the eastern sky. The French gunners would have no time to consider the beauty of the spectacle, though. Already they were bustling about the huge gun, directed by a small plump officer who waved his arms a good deal. The screeched orders came faintly to the ears of the men concealed on the hill. Septimus focused his telescope for a good look at the officer. He wore a large cocked hat, and there was a curious appearance about his face which Septimus could not at first explain. Then he realised what it was. The French officer sported a magnificent black moustache which curled right to his ears.

But now the gunners were elevating the monster gun. He saw the red spark of the match as a man blew it into life and the disciplined movement of the gunners stepping one pace back with the recoil lines. Then from the great muzzle of Terrible Jack darted a long jet of orange flame and a spreading cloud of smoke. The thunder of the big gun's discharge followed quickly. The signal for the attack on Fort Flambeau had been given.

3

'Wait!' snapped Lieutenant Pyke as his seamen started to move. 'I'll give the word!'

The short interval gave Septimus time to note that the shot from Jean le Terrible had raised a white fountain of water just short of the frigate and somewhat to one side. Then he was watching excitedly as half-a-dozen of Salter's Marines, crouching and darting forward from bush to bush, reached the bottom of the hill and started across the open valley towards the gate of the fort. Four of them had small kegs slung on their backs. The northern walls of the fort were deserted – the attention of the defenders was given entirely to the result of their giant gun's shooting. But would the Marines reach the gate without being seen?

Septimus was unable to see what happened, for when the four redcoats were still a hundred paces from the gate Mr Pyke gave the order to advance.

Down the uneven slope of the hill they came, as silently as speed would allow, using such cover as the thorn-bushes gave. Charles Barry was just in front of Septimus, and Lieutenant Pyke's epauletted shoulders could be seen in front of Charles. At the heels of Midshipman Quinn came Tod Beamish, a canvas bag slung from his broad shoulders. Forty men descending a limestone hill-side could hardly help making considerable noise no matter how careful they were, but a glance showed Septimus that the fort had not yet observed their approach. The giant gun bellowed once again as they gained the level ground at the foot of the hill.

The red coats of the six Marines were now clustered right under the big wooden gate of the fort. They would be placing their kegs of gunpowder close against it and lighting the fuses. As the seamen, obeying Pyke's gesture, spread out and began to race for the gate, Septimus caught a glimpse of Mr Gifford's men breaking from cover some distance away on their left.

The sprinting men, cutlass in hand, were halfway to the gate before those in the fort noticed their approach. A chorus of yells told them that they had been seen – but like an angry reply to the alarmed shouts came a shattering explosion. The Marines had exploded their mine under the gate.

'Run, you lubbers! Run!' roared Pyke at the top of his powerful voice.

Septimus, panting up the slight slope in the first group of attackers, saw heads appearing on the ramparts above as if by magic. One or two scattered musket-shots rang out, hitting no one. He saw, too, that the timbers of the gate had been rent, but not completely shattered, by the gunpowder explosion. Then the whole party was across the open ground and under the north wall of Fort Flambeau. The *Althea*'s feint approach had allowed her landing-parties to reach the fort without being subjected to cannon-fire from the embrasures, and now the guns on the walls above could not bear on them.

'Axes here!' shouted Mr Pyke, pointing with his sword towards the half-broken gate.

Three seamen leapt forward to strike at the sagging timbers. But the delay was dangerous in the extreme. From the French soldiers on the walls each side of the gate came a volley of musketry. A seaman at Septimus's side fell, shot through the head, and others were wounded. A distant cheering told that Gifford's men and the Marines were attacking to east and west of them, but meanwhile the party attacking the gate would be wiped out unless the gate yielded – and it was still resisting the axemen.

Septimus looked round. 'Beamish!' he called. 'Out with them!'

The big seaman swiftly opened his bag, allowing four round objects with tags of fuse attached to roll on the ground. Septimus took the flint and steel from him and lit a short length of slow-match.

'Look out!' Barry called urgently. 'Here's another volley!'

'You're a cricketer, Charles,' returned Septimus coolly. 'See what you can do with these balls.'

He touched his slow-match to two of the shells. Barry, with a puzzled glance at him, took one of them as it was handed to him. Above the shouting and the crashing of the axes the second volley rang out. Mr Quinn's cocked hat sailed from his head, and Beamish gave a loud exclamation.

'Got me left arm, sir – it's nothing,' he said, and took the other shell with its spluttering fuse.

'Drop it just over the top, Charles,' directed the junior midshipman.

The two iron balls sailed up into the air with their short fuses whirling and sparking. Barry's soared truly, to fall only a few feet behind the line of defenders. Beamish's mightier throw carried well over the ramparts.

'What in the name of goodness are they, Sep?' demanded Barry. 'Nothing seems to have happened.'

'Pray wait and see,' was Mr Quinn's reply. 'And stand by for a third volley.'

Under the savage blows of the axes the gate was beginning to yield. Some of the seamen had brought up a great boulder and were hurling it against the timbers. The two Marines who had not carried powder-kegs were bringing their muskets into play against the enemy. If muzzle-loading muskets had not taken such a time to reload, the besiegers would have been mown down by a third and more accurate volley as they surged impatiently round the gate, and the defenders would have been free to concentrate on the two parties who were assaulting the walls.

But something disturbing was taking place overhead on the ramparts. Before the French soldiers had withdrawn their ramrods after ramming down charge and bullet, they were all aware of the thick black smoke that eddied round them, emanating from the two iron balls that had been hurtled over their heads from below. That smoke, or gas, spread like magic in the still air, and as its evil stench came to each man's nostrils he began to cough and choke.

Those below could see the vapour rising above the heads of the enemy. Mr Preece, appearing unexpectedly at Septimus's side, was chuckling delightly as he lit the fuse of another shell.

'Little Jim's the medicine for Boney, yess indeed!' said he, and the two remaining balls, hurled by himself and the junior midshipman, pitched into the fort.

The noise of coughing was loud enough to rival the shouts of the seamen at the gate. A voice above screamed the order to fire just as the gate timbers began to give way, and the volley that came from the muskets of Frenchmen whose eyes were streaming water and whose convulsive coughing spoiled their aim was a ragged one indeed. The seamen, learning wisdom from the first volleys, had scattered, and only a few musket-balls found their mark.

One of them, by ill fortune, lodged in the shoulder of Charles Barry, knocking him to the ground. But he picked himself up and, with his left arm hanging limply at his side, joined the charge through the gate. For now the way was open – or so it seemed.

Lieutenant Pyke, charging through the gap in the splintered timbers at the head of his men, suddenly turned and flung them back with a roar of '*Grape! Cover!*'

The French commander, a man of resource, had shifted one of his lighter cannon from the walls to command the ramp inside the gate, and – as the First Lieutenant had guessed – he had loaded it with grape-shot. The gun thundered and its charge screamed down the ramp, rattling against the broken gate. But thanks to Pyke's prompt action and bull-like roar the narrow space was clear of attackers and only one man, caught as he darted round into cover, was hurt.

Next moment Pyke was leading the men back up the ramp. The gunners had no time to reload before the cheering, shouting seamen were upon them. Septimus had managed to get close behind the First Lieutenant for that second charge, and came up on to the flat area inside the ramparts at Pyke's heels. A piercing whistle cut across the noise of conflict – the agreed signal to Captain Salter that the main gate had fallen. The sound was followed by a ragged volley from the rank of Frenchmen who had fallen back as the British gained the ramparts. Not a single shot of that volley appeared to take effect, and it was small wonder. For the area within the ramparts was filled with a black and choking vapour.

As the men of the *Althea* ran forward brandishing their cutlasses they, too, were coughing and choking, with watering eyes and crimson faces.

'By Hector!' wheezed Lieutenant Pyke, pausing in his stride. 'The dogs have fired their magazine!'

'No, by your leave, sir – it's that!' Septimus, his eyes streaming, pointed to a smoking ball of iron that lay a few feet away. 'Smoke bomb, sir!'

Pyke spared a glare for him and then continued his rush.

The scene on the ramparts was a strange one. Half-visible through the curling wreaths of smoke, seamen and soldiers clashed with cutlass and pistol and sword, for the French were resisting gallantly. But instead of British cheers and French cries of *Vive la France!* there was one universal uproar of coughing, choking, wheezing and gasping.

Septimus caught a glimpse of Charles Barry, with his left arm hanging helpless, lunging with his cutlass at a French soldier. But Midshipman Quinn had checked his advance before he came to grips with an enemy. He had plans of his own. Dodging the smoke and the lurching, struggling figures, he came round the flank of the skirmish and suddenly emerged into a clearer atmosphere. For a second he paused to wipe the moisture from his eyes and send a quick glance round him.

On his left were the eastern ramparts, where Gifford's men, having hurled grapnels over the wall, had swarmed up the ropes to gain a footing on the walls in spite of determined resistance. The gunners, abandoning Jean le Terrible to deal with this dangerous foe, were aiding their comrades to beat off a savage attack led by red-headed Fitzroy Cocker. And standing apart from the conflict to scream oaths and encouragement at his men was the plump officer, the commandant of the fort.

Septimus took one look at those wonderful moustachios and ran at the commandant, cutlass in hand. From behind him came Tod Beamish's gasping shout.

'I'm with you, sir!'

Midshipman Quinn did not check his rapid advance. The French officer whirled to meet him, his own sword raised. As the midshipman's cutlass swept down, the sword deflected it in a glancing parry and Septimus only avoided the quick riposte by a lightning spring to one side.

'Stand clear!' he cried as Beamish, coming up to his assistance, showed signs of tackling the commandant himself.

Again the blades clashed, while Beamish spun round to ward off any interference. But the little duel was not observed by men who were too hard-pressed themselves to spare a thought or a glance for their leader. Septimus had some little knowledge of swordplay, but the Frenchman's lighter weapon was far more rapid in use than his heavy cutlass. All he could do for some moments was to parry the commandant's dangerous thrusts and step back and back as the French officer pressed him. The plump man's eyes were gleaming and he showed his white teeth below that splendid moustache.

'Aha, my little Englishman!' he snarled. 'I have you!'

Since he was not an inch taller than Septimus himself, his use of the word 'little' annoyed the midshipman exceedingly. And the even-tempered Mr Quinn was dangerous when aroused. Also, he had set his heart on those moustachios.

'Come and get me, then, monsieur!' he retorted, and whirled up his cutlass, leaving his body unguarded.

With a cry of triumph his adversary lunged straight for the midshipman's breast, but Septimus, who had gambled on that immediate thrust and timed his own movement accordingly, swung his middle body to the left in the nick of time. The commandant's blade passed so close to his right side that it pierced his coat. And before it could withdraw Septimus had brought his sword-arm down like a clamp, pinning the weapon to his side, while his clenched left fist took the Frenchman hard under the chin. The man reeled backwards, loosing his sword.

'Hold him, Beamish!' panted the midshipman, thrusting his cutlass into his belt.

The seaman was behind the commandant in an instant and from behind him caught both arms in a grip of iron. Septimus felt in his pocket and pulled out his scissors.

The commandant screamed as his triumphant adversary, his eyes gleaming, advanced upon him with scissors outstretched.

'*Dieu-de-dieu!*' he quavered. 'Will you take my life with so barbarous a weapon?'

'Pray don't distress yourself, monsieur,' returned Septimus. 'It is not your life that I require.'

And he raised the scissors.

4

Far out in the blue of the Mediterranean a flutter of coloured bunting ran up to the yardarm of the *Althea* and was seen by the watchful Mr Preece, who had been posted by Lieutenant Pyke with a telescope on the seaward ramparts of the captured fort. Mr Preece read the signal and reported it to the First Lieutenant.

'Relieving force advancing along the coast from northward. Retire immediately.'

The work they had come to do had been done. Taken between two forces, and with Salter's Marines arriving to add to their discomfiture, the garrison of the fort had surrendered just as Septimus had disarmed their commandant. The Frenchmen were herded into their barracks and locked in, and the work of demolition began at once. With Tod Beamish's immense strength doing most of the work in spite of a flesh-wound in his arm, small parties of seamen hoisted the smaller cannon on to the ramparts and pushed them over to crash down to the rocks below. Jean le Terrible was much too heavy to deal with in this way, but they had unseated the giant gun from its carriage, smashed the lock mechanism, and spiked the touch-hole. It would be many weeks before Terrible Jack could be fired again.

Finally, when the frigate's signal reached them, they lit a long fuse which Mr Preece had been preparing and marched rapidly away from the fort. Scarcely had they gained the hillside when a mighty explosion shook the ground beneath them and a towering mushroom of black smoke showed that the magazine had been well and truly blown up. The raid on Fort Flambeau had been an unqualified success. Three seamen and a marine had been killed, and a score of men had minor wounds – including Charles Barry, whose shoulder had been roughly bandaged by Mr Preece. But the French had once again been taught that so long as Britain held command of the seas the ten-to-one man-power of Napoleon Bonaparte could not hold off the daring islanders.

Back over the rough hills filed the raiding force and down the stream-gorge to their boats. Only one man among them was far from cheerful, and that was the French commandant, who was being taken on board the *Althea* as prisoner.

It was after noon when the four boats sighted the frigate bearing up to southward of them. The weary men cheered as they pulled the last of the distance back to their floating home and a long-delayed meal. Some four hours later Midshipman Septimus Quinn was summoned to the main cabin, the message being brought by a pale and anxious-looking Barry.

'Oh, my shoulder's all right,' he answered in reply to his friend's question. 'It's you I'm worried about. Pyke's furious, and the captain's looking solemn. Better cram on all sail to the cabin, Sep – and good luck!'

Septimus hastened along the deck, passing the scowling Lieutenant Pyke on the way, and found Captain Sainsbury alone in the cabin, sitting at the table. He looked up with a frown as the junior midshipman stood before him at attention.

'Mr Quinn,' he said severely, 'you are making a nuisance of yourself. I hardly know what to do with you. Mr Pyke has just reported to me that you endangered the success of the assault on Fort Flambeau by using, without permission, some kind of infernal machine. He has requested a Court Martial.'

Septimus swallowed hard. This was serious indeed, even though it was unfair. He remained rigid and silent.

'On the other hand,' continued the captain, eyeing him sharply, 'Mr Gifford states that the French defence was demoralised by a choking vapour, and Mr Barry asserts that had it not been for this vapour the third volley from the walls would have prevented the gate from being forced. I gather that four iron shells were flung over the ramparts at your instruction. What were they?'

'A little experiment, sir,' replied Septimus deprecatingly. 'The shells were stuffed with cotton-waste impregnated with a solution of sulphur with various acids, and—'

'Mr Quinn!' snapped the captain. 'You will in future make no little experiments in the course of a difficult raid. You understand?'

'Aye aye, sir,' murmured the midshipman.

'And there is something more, Mr Quinn. The French commandant, a gentleman, as he informs me, of high family, claims that he was grossly insulted and maltreated by you. He asserts – er – in short, you – ah – removed his – er – moustachios.'

The captain seemed to have some difficulty in getting the words out. Septimus, his face reddening, looked at the deck.

'Well, sir?' demanded his superior sharply. 'Did you or did you not disarm this officer in single combat and then cut off his moustache?'

'I did, sir.' The midshipman felt in his pocket and produced a folded sheet of paper. 'I have the moustaches here, sir.'

Captain Sainsbury passed a hand swiftly across the lower part of his face before leaning forward to inspect the two curling lengths of black hair.

'And why, may I ask, did you perform this – this dastardly act?' he inquired harshly, still hiding his mouth with his hand.

'I wished to send them to – to a lady,' mumbled Septimus,

blushing a rich tomato-colour. Then he looked up and met the captain's eye. 'I wish, sir,' he added, 'to claim them as spoils of war.'

'Oh, you do?' Again Captain Sainsbury had difficulty in speaking. 'Hum. I must confess I see no use in returning them to their – er – owner. Now attend to me, Mr Quinn. You are under my serious displeasure. You will report to Mr Pyke for extra duty every day for a week. That's all.'

'Aye aye, sir.' Septimus saluted and turned to go.

'And Mr Quinn.'

'Yes, sir?'

'Next time you go ashore, you will leave smoke-bombs and knight-errantry behind you – and scissors.'

Mr Quinn, vastly relieved at being let off so lightly, returned to the midshipmen's berth to continue the formal letter he was composing to Miss Philippa Barry to accompany a handsome pair of French moustachios 'which, I am informed, you have expressed a desire to possess'. But he was puzzled as well as relieved. For as he had closed the main cabin door behind him he had heard a curious noise from within. The *Althea*'s crew declared that their captain seldom smiled and never laughed. Had it not been for this, Midshipman Quinn would have sworn that Captain Sainsbury, alone in his cabin, was roaring with merriment.

Chapter Six

Captain Septimus

1

The armed brig *Blanche* was as French as her name and as daring as a Frenchman might be expected to be. For, with Nelson and his warships only fifteen miles away to eastward, off Toulon, the *Blanche* had ventured out of her small home port of Quelles to carry a full cargo of fruit and vegetables to the market in Marseilles. On this brilliant morning of 25th September 1803 she was scudding along before a fresh breeze almost out of sight of the land on her starboard beam. Her decks were gleaming, for she had been washed-down at sunrise, and gleaming also were the four small six-pounder cannon that stood in their lashings two on either side of the deck. The owner and captain of the *Blanche* liked to see things clean and shining, for she was a girl.

Jeanne Terray was her name, and she was sixteen years old. When her father had died, leaving the brig to his only daughter, Jeanne had left her studies in Toulon (where she had learned, among other things, to sing and to speak English) and had taken charge of the little vessel. The grey-haired mate, Joseph Lebas, looked after the navigation and other sea matters, but Jeanne ordered the brig's voyages and arranged her cargoes. She was an outspoken young lady and declared that she didn't care whether Napoleon Bonaparte or King Louis ruled France so long as the *Blanche* was permitted to voyage as she wished; which shocked Joseph, who was an ardent supporter of Napoleon. As for the English, Jeanne snapped her slim fingers at them.

'You run a risk, mademoiselle,' Joseph had warned her when they left Quelles. 'There's a rumour that an English frigate is raiding along this coast.'

'Bah!' the girl had replied with a toss of her long black hair. 'I can talk to this English ship if she crosses my course!'

'Your English, mademoiselle, may not convince a real Englishman.'

'I didn't mean I'd talk English, fool!' she had snapped at him. 'I meant I would talk with those.'

And she had pointed to her four small guns.

This morning Jeanne was standing on the low poop of the little vessel, sniffing the keen salt air. With her black locks bound beneath a red handkerchief, her blue skirt and loose grey trousers, she looked like a handsome pirate. The *Blanche*, she noticed, was not really moving very fast through the water in spite of the flurry of foam she was making in her progress westward. That was because she was carrying as much cargo as her holds would contain. She had just made this observation when the lookout high on the brig's stumpy mainmast hailed her.

'Captain Jeanne! Sail right ahead! Looks like a warship – a frigate!'

Joseph, who had heard, came running aft, his plump face pale and anxious.

'We must run for the land, mademoiselle!' he cried. 'This can only be the English frigate I warned you of!'

Jeanne hesitated. Her impulse was to hold on her course, and fight if she had to. But that would be the sheerest foolishness – and besides, there were men in her crew whom she had known from childhood.

'Put her on the larboard tack,' she snapped at the helmsman.

The *Blanche* wallowed round and turned her bows northward, heading for the coast that was no more than a thin brown line on the horizon. There was, she remembered, no port or coastal defences on that section of coast, but presumably the English ship – if she was English – would not dare to come any nearer to an enemy shore.

It soon appeared that Jeanne was mistaken. The vessel ahead, now in plain view from the deck, had altered course to steer diagonally in towards the land. More than that. She was heading so as to cross the brig's course and intercept her, and she was obviously a very fast sailer.

'Joseph!' shouted Jeanne. 'Hoist the spritsail – quickly!'

It was the one sail unset, that small square of canvas that could be set on the bowsprit, and it would make little difference to the speed of the heavily-laden brig, but the brig's captain was not the girl to leave anything untried that could help her in the race. The mate repeated the order. Two of the nine seamen who formed the *Blanche*'s crew jumped to obey. Joseph came up to her, wringing his hands.

'We'll never get clear,' he moaned. 'If only we were nearer Marseilles – there's a fort there—'

'Stop whining, man!' she told him. 'We're not near Marseilles, so that's that. We'll have to stand on our own feet. Take off the lashings and have the guns run out.'

'But—'

Jeanne stamped her foot in its heavy seaboot. 'Do as I say! Do you think I've had the men trained in gunnery for nothing?'

Joseph, shaking his head miserably, trotted for'ard. The girl stared across the sparkling blue of the Mediterranean to where the intercepting vessel flew like a swallow across the waves. There was no doubt now that she was a British frigate, with main, royal, and topsails set in a pyramid of gleaming white canvas. She was a lovely sight even to Jeanne's wrathful gaze – wrathful because she held that these waters were hers, to trade in as she wished without interference from Englishmen – and she was certainly making twice the speed of the *Blanche*. So swiftly were the two ships drawing together that the frigate seemed to grow larger every few seconds. She was near enough now for the girl captain to see the British colours go sailing up to her yardarm. There was no possibility of escape for the brig.

Down on the deck the two six-pounders on the larboard side were loaded and ready, their three-man crews standing by with a smoking linstock each. Jeanne set her jaw firmly. She was no admirer of Napoleon Bonaparte, but this was a matter of France against England. She would fight.

Even as she opened her mouth to shout to the gunners to stand by, a single puff of white smoke burst from the flank of the English ship. A cable's length ahead of the brig a shining fountain of white water rose from the blue surface. That was the signal to heave-to. Ignoring Joseph's spread hands and imploring face, Jeanne folded her arms and ordered her helmsman to hold his course. The penalty, she knew, was that the next shot from the frigate would be aimed at her. Again she found she was mistaken. A second puff of smoke resulted in another fountain exactly the same distance ahead of the *Blanche* and a moment later a third ball performed just the same feat. After which the rapidly-closing frigate ceased fire.

Jeanne flushed. The English were playing with her, treating her ship as a thing unworthy of their cannon-balls. Well, they should see.

Nearer and nearer came the two ships on their converging courses until the frigate was less than a quarter of a mile from her victim. Seen across the narrowing space of blue water she was a lovely and threatening sight with her black hull and its broad band of white where the open gun-ports yawned, her towering sails, and the thirty-five-foot bowsprit thrusting like a fencer's foil above the froth of white water at her forefoot. Jeanne set her teeth.

'Bear off,' she told the helmsman. 'Keep her there.'

The brig was now running parallel to the frigate.

'Stand by to fire!'

As the girl shouted the preparatory order, Joseph rushed to the larboard guns, waving his arms frenziedly.

'No!' he shrieked. 'Louis – Gaston – I command you not to fire! The Englishman will blow us out of the water!'

'Tais-toi!' Jeanne hurled at him. And then, at the top of her voice, *'Tirez!'*

Louis and his gun's crew did not obey. But Gaston, a tall youth who was Jeanne's devoted admirer, touched his linstock to the touch-hole. The little six-pounder belched smoke and flame. Jeanne, peering above the smoke to see the result, thought she saw white splinters fly from the frigate's side just above the line of gun-ports. But before the smoke had cleared the frigate replied – not the full broadside which Joseph had prophesied, but a single shot as before. This time, however, the ball did not fall ahead of the *Blanche*. It was aimed high to hit mast or spars, and though it struck neither it served its purpose by severing halyards and rigging on the brig's foremast.

Down came sail and yard with a flap and a crash. The *Blanche* spun round, heeling madly as the balance of her sails was upset, and came up into the wind to lie helpless. As if copying her action, the frigate spun neatly round, to lie hove-to a cable's length away.

Jeanne had dashed to the weather rail where her father's old dress-sword hung in its sheath of gilt leather.

'All hands stand by to repel boarders!' she cried, drawing the narrow blade and waving it aloft.

She was a gallant if somewhat futile figure, straddling there on the poop with the sunlight flashing from her sword and glinting on the gold earrings that hung below the fringe of the red handkerchief. Only Gaston showed any sign of responding to her order. The rest of the crew abandoned their guns and, shrugging their shoulders, began to gather in the flapping canvas of the dismantled sail. As for Joseph, he ran on to the poop without a glance for Jeanne and slashed through the flag halyards with his knife. The French colours fluttered down to the deck. The *Blanche* had surrendered.

For a moment it seemed that Jeanne would leap upon Joseph with her sword. She took an angry pace forward, and so furious was her look that the grey-haired mate literally shook at the knees. But the girl controlled herself and spat one word at him.

'Coward!'

Then she turned away to stare despairingly at the English ship.

The wind had brought the frigate nearer to her prey. An officer leaped on to her rail, steadying himself by the shrouds, and shouted through a speaking-trumpet. His French was bad but understandable.

'Brig ahoy! We accept your surrender. Give your name, cargo, and destination.'

Joseph replied, making a funnel of his hands.

'Brig *Blanche*, bound for Marseilles with fresh fruit and vegetables!'

Jeanne, who would have stopped him had she been able, bit her lip and clenched her small brown hand on the hilt of the sword. To deny that she had surrendered would be to make a fool of herself. She must accept the fact that her mate and crew were against her, though it was mutiny on their part.

On board the frigate the officer was reporting that reply to his captain. In a few moments he hailed the brig again.

'Brig there! We are sending a prize crew on board.'

That was all. Not even a warning to try no tricks on pain of receiving a broadside. That was like the arrogant English, Jeanne told herself bitterly – taking it for granted that their superiority could not be challenged. It was galling to watch the orderly bustle on board the frigate as a boat was swung out from the davits and lowered. Men slid down the ropes into the boat and in a matter of seconds were pulling towards the brig. They were coming to take her ship from her.

Jeanne's dark eyes glittered with something that was not anger. With an impetuous gesture she flung the sword far out across the water in the direction of the approaching boat. It flashed in the sun before it disappeared for ever. If she could not strike a blow, at least she would not give up her sword to the English.

The frigate's boat came neatly alongside, and Jeanne scowled down at the brown faces and tarry pigtails of the English sailors. There was a boy in the sternsheets of the boat, but a hasty glance showed her no officer. However, she would have to receive her conquerors with proper nautical courtesy. She went down from the poop to the head of the ladder which Louis and her men had slung over, and stood waiting with head thrown back and hands clasped behind her.

A cocked hat, topping a grave and somewhat owlish face, appeared above the rail and the boy she had seen in the boat stepped on board. His keen glance passed over the girl and round the little circle of scowling French seamen.

'I wish to speak with the captain of this vessel,' he said in careful French.

Jeanne, smiling scornfully, took a pace forward.

'I am the captain of this vessel,' she said, in English.

She had expected the boy to look surprised, but he merely bowed.

'Your servant, mademoiselle,' he said. 'I am Midshipman Septimus Quinn, of His Majesty's frigate *Althea*.'

2

The circumstances which gave Midshipman Quinn his first command were these. The *Althea* had been making a series of landings to complete her daring survey of the coastal defences west of Toulon. She was to report to Lord Nelson off Toulon on 30th September, and her difficult task was nearly finished. Two of these landings had met with opposition, for it was now common knowledge along the shores of Provence that a British frigate was cruising and raiding on that coast, and in the skirmishing Mr Haswell, the Third Lieutenant, had been killed by a musket-ball and Mr Gifford wounded in the leg, though not severely. With Midshipman Cocker acting in place of both second and third lieutenants and Midshipman Barry still unable to use his left arm, the only officer Captain Sainsbury could spare for command of a prize was Septimus Quinn.

The *Althea* herself was in sore need of fresh greens and fruit and Nelson's blockading squadrons off Toulon must be in the same plight, so that it was the brig's cargo that had decided Captain Sainsbury to make a prize of her and take her into Toulon.

'Mr Quinn,' he had said in giving the midshipman his orders, 'you will take six seamen, make such arrangements on board the brig as seem good to you, and shape a course for Toulon, a course that will take you out of sight of the coast. I shall be taking the *Althea* closer inshore tonight, and later standing southward, so we shall not sail in company. But I propose to be off Toulon on the 30th, by which date I shall expect you to have reported to the flagship, disposed of your cargo, and found quarters for your men. Good fortune to you, Mr Quinn.'

And so Septimus had hurriedly collected his gear and his men (among whom was the huge Tod Beamish) and put off for the *Blanche*. He had seen the sword flung from the brig's poop as the boat approached. He had intended to receive the captain's sword, the customary symbol of surrender, and then to hand it back to him with a graceful bow and a few well-chosen words, for he had admired the courage with which the little ship had fired on the frigate even though it was a hopeless gesture. It annoyed him to be deprived of this courteous act, and – though he had not shown it – he was taken aback to find that the captain was a girl, and a pretty girl as well.

The six men of the prize crew had clambered on board after him. The *Althea*'s boat was pulling back to the frigate. He was alone, in command of an armed brig, with half-a-dozen seamen and eleven prisoners to dispose of. He turned away from Jeanne to face his men, his mind seething with the orders that must be given at once.

'Beamish, you're appointed second-in-command. Take Frith and Eccles and get all these Frenchmen secured in the forecastle. Search the place for arms first, and see that the men are unarmed.'

'Aye aye, sir.'

Septimus addressed Jeanne. 'Mademoiselle, pray tell your men that at the first sign of resistance they will be shot. My men, as you see are all armed with musket or pistol.'

'I shall say nothing to them! cried the girl angrily, folding her arms.

'As you please, mademoiselle,' Septimus replied coolly, and

mustered his halting French. '*Vous, Français, si cous montrez quelque résistance, mes matelots vous ferez morts, vitement! Comprenez?*'

It was obvious that his meaning was clear to the Frenchmen. One or two of them grinned widely at the midshipman's efforts in their language. Beamish and his two assistants shepherded them towards the forehatch.

'Dobbs! Reave those flag-halyards and hoist British colours,' was Mr Quinn's next order, followed by a command to Wallace and O'Neill to make temporary repairs to the fore-rigging and get the foresail hoisted.

The seamen ran to execute these instructions, leaving Septimus and Jeanne Terray facing each other alone. The girl's flushed defiant face made a contrast to the midshipman's calm but somewhat puzzled countenance.

'Your name, mademoiselle, if you please?' he asked.

'Jeanne Terray. Why do they send you on board my ship instead of a man?'

'I obey my orders, mademoiselle,' returned Septimus, unmoved. 'I cannot ask you to give up your sword, since I saw you fling it away. But I do not wish to confine you in your cabin. If you will give me your parole, your sword of honour that you will take no action of any kind against me or my seamen, you will be free—'

'I will not give it!' Jeanne cried, stamping her booted foot. 'Why should I? You English pirates attacked a merchant ship – a harmless brig carrying a harmless cargo. You are not men of honour to whom I would give my parole!'

Septimus raised his eyebrows. 'You must remember, mademoiselle, that my country is at war with yours,' he remarked. 'As for your ship being harmless, there is a nasty hole in the bulwarks of the *Althea*, made by a six-pounder ball. I must remind you that we only fired to disable your rigging after you had refused to heave-to.'

'So, because you were the stronger, I ought to have given in without firing a shot!' she flashed. 'I tell you, Monsieur

Midshipman, I would have fought you to the last if my mate had not surrendered against my orders!'

'Your mate was wise, mademoiselle. All the same, you will allow me to say that I admire your courage in resisting—'

'I do not want your admiration!'

Jeanne turned her back on him. Septimus was scratching his head and wondering what to do with her when Beamish came trotting up to him.

'Prisoners snug and safe, sir,' he reported. 'No weapons, sir, and I've rigged a beam across the forecastle door.'

'Very good, Mr Beamish.'

Septimus was about to add further orders when Dobbs, squat and black-whiskered, hurried to him from the poop to report the flag-halyards reaved and the British colours hoisted.

'*Althea*'s off, sir,' he added. 'Dippin' her ensign – see it?'

Septimus spun round in time to see the frigate's colours dipping in salute as she went about on her new course.

'Then dip our own colours, man – quickly!' he snapped. 'This is a British prize, and we—'

He broke off as O'Neill's fiery red head appeared at his elbow.

'Misther Quinn, sir,' said the Irishman breathlessly, 'the fores'l yard's cracked in smithereens, and not a spar can we find to use instead.'

A second later Eccles, an undersized London River seaman, bobbed up on the midshipman's other side.

'Please, sir – the prisoners, sir,' he squeaked. 'They're a-shoutin' for food, sir – ain't 'ad no breakfast, sir, so they says.'

'My men must be fed!' put in Jeanne angrily.

'Plenty o' nice raw cabbages on board,' suggested Dobbs with a grin. 'Maybe they'd relish some—'

'That's enough!' The midshipman's voice had an edge to it. 'Why haven't you obeyed my order? Step lively, Dobbs, or I'll have you in irons! You, O'Neill, get that yard rigged. Lash two sweeps from the longboat yonder if you can't find a spar. Eccles! This lady will show you where the brig's pantry is. One loaf, or

The brig *Blanche*, captain (for one day) Septimus Quinn.

two rounds of hard tack, to each Frenchman, and a pannikin of water.'

'I refuse—' began Jeanne.

'You'll obey, or your men will go hungry,' he told her sternly. 'Mr Beamish, go with them. When the food's issued, lock Mademoiselle Terray in her cabin. She declines to give her parole. Look sharp, now!'

The men scattered at his rapid fire of orders. Jeanne shook off Beamish's arm and led the way, throwing a furious glance over her shoulder at Septimus. Mr Quinn, left alone, mopped his brow with his handkerchief. He had experienced his first taste of a captain's responsibility and found it a little trying. He felt thankful that the *Blanche*'s voyage to the fleet off Toulon would not be a long one.

The *Blanche*, with her sails flapping, was still yawing about in the breeze. He hurried aft, to the helm, and steadied her, leaving Dobbs to keep her to the wind until the foresail could be rigged again. Then for'ard, to see that O'Neill and Wallace, with Frith to help them, were getting on with the work. On the way along the deck he caught sight of the six-pounders swinging to the ship's roll. Those would have to be made fast before the brig got under way – and there was surely a long spar lashed under the bulwarks between the guns? Examination showed it to be a jury-topmast. Of course, neither the featherbrained O'Neill nor the slow-witted Wallace had thought of looking there for a spar.

Five minutes later he had Frith cutting down the spar for a new yard while Wallace and O'Neill spliced the severed rigging, Eccles and Dobbs securing the guns, and Beamish at the helm ready to receive the course for sailing. Septimus hurried below to find chart and dividers, hoping that they would not be in Mademoiselle Terray's cabin, where she was locked in. He had no wish to hold further conversation with that difficult young lady.

The second cabin he entered – he guessed it was the mate's – had a chart pinned on a small table. It did not take him long to estimate the brig's present position and decide on his course. Up to the deck he raced again, slackening his pace to a more dignified walk as he approached the poop.

'Course due south, Mr Beamish,' he said, 'when she's fully rigged again. I'm going to stay on that course until nightfall and then make eastward.'

'Aye aye, sir,' returned Beamish. 'If this easterly wind holds,' he added, 'we'll be beating up against it all the way to Toulon, sir.'

From for'ard came Frith's hail. 'Fores'l all ready for h'isting, sir!'

'Hoist away!' shouted Septimus.

The canvas ran up, flapping from its new yard, and bellied out in the wind. Beamish put the helm gently over.

'Main and fore braces!'

As the yards were hauled back the *Blanche* caught the wind and heeled slightly. Then she was ploughing slowly through the water on her southward course, the first leg of her voyage towards Toulon, and her new captain could spare a glance for the ship he had left. The *Althea* was already a small white speck on the northern horizon, standing in towards the enemy coast and the last of her daring reconnaissances. Mr Midshipman Quinn fought down the feeling of loneliness that came suddenly upon him and turned his mind to the work in hand.

The *Blanche* was shipshape and under way, but he had still much to do. Beamish could be trusted to see that the men were at their proper stations. Meanwhile, it was Mr Quinn's task to examine the brig's papers and cargo lists – and those were almost certainly in the captain's cabin, where Jeanne Terray was imprisoned.

It had to be done. He went below, and making his way aft to the stern cabin unlocked the door. Though it was the largest cabin in the ship, the stern cabin was very small compared with Captain Sainsbury's cabin in the *Althea*. It was lit by a window in the stern and furnished with seat-lockers, cupboards, and a small table. Jeanne was sitting at the table facing the door, with her face hidden in her hands. At the midshipman's entrance she hastily lowered her hands and lifted her head defiantly.

'Pray pardon my intrusion, mademoiselle,' Septimus said politely, 'but I have to ask you for the *Blanche*'s cargo lists.'

'And if I decline to give them?' she countered.

'Then you will put me to the trouble of searching this cabin for them, mademoiselle.' He noticed that the girl's hands had gone below the table, as if to a drawer there. 'I fancy,' he added, 'the papers I require are in the drawer.'

'They are,' said Jeanne between her clenched teeth. 'And so is – this!'

She made a swift movement, and Septimus found himself looking into the muzzle of a pistol, at a range of three feet. Inwardly he cursed his folly in not making certain that the girl was unarmed. Outwardly he remained quite composed. The click as the pistol was cocked sounded very menacing.

'I gave no parole,' Jeanne said exultingly. 'Your life is now in my hands, Monsieur Midshipman.' She rose to her feet. 'You will walk in front of me to the forecastle, making no outcry, and release my crew. Otherwise – I shall shoot, be certain of that!'

Midshipman Quinn's eyes met hers steadily. He did not move.

'Mademoiselle,' he said calmly. 'I shall do no such thing and you will not shoot. You have too much sense.'

'Why should I not pull the trigger now, monsieur?' she cried threateningly.

'Because, mademoiselle, the noise of the report would bring my men here at once. You would kill me, but they might very well kill you – and your crew – in revenge. Give me that pistol, please.'

Without moving his gaze from her he reached slowly for the weapon. For a moment he thought she would pull the trigger, so furious were her eyes. Then they wavered and fell. He grasped the pistol by the barrel just as she let it fall. Next moment she had flung herself on the seat under the stern-window, sobbing wildly.

Mr Quinn uncocked the pistol and dropped it into his pocket before rummaging in the drawer and finding the lists he wanted. Then he made a rapid but thorough search for any other aggressive weapons, without finding any. Finally he addressed the unheeding figure on the window seat.

'Your supper will be served at sunset, mademoiselle. You will no doubt excuse me from joining you.'

With that he went out, locking the door behind him.

A study of the *Blanche*'s cargo-lists confirmed that she was carrying a very full cargo of vegetables and fruit, as well as a few other packages. One of the latter, he noticed with amusement, was listed as 'Bale Seventeen, Theatrical Costumes for Marseilles'. It was an item he was to remember later, in strange circumstances. There were also several boxes of fresh eggs. He went to find Eccles, who had been assistant cook in the frigate.

At sunset precisely a very hungry Jeanne, sitting resignedly at her table, heard the lock of her cabin door click. A wizened and grinning seaman entered with a tray whose contents steamed and smelt delicious.

' 'Ere's a honion homelette, miss, a melon an' sugar, an' a glass o' wine,' he said. 'Also one pistol, hunloaded – all with the compliments of Mr Septimus Quinn.'

3

An hour after sunset the east wind freshened. By four bells in the first watch it was blowing half-a-gale, and the brig *Blanche* was tossing and plunging under shortened sail. There was no rest for her prize crew that night, and it was not until near dawn that Midshipman Quinn noted a sudden change in wind direction. The driving gusts ceased, the sea became a smooth and heaving black surface instead of a series of white-fanged waves, and as the first faint light grew there spread around the tossing vessel a grey haze that hung low on the waters.

Septimus went down to the mate's cabin and lit the oil-lamp. He had been unable to alter course during that stormy night, but the brig must be at least twenty miles out from the coast now, and with the wind veered to south he could make eastward for Toulon. He put on his spectacles and pored over the chart, trying to estimate what position his ship had reached. The gale must have blown him well to westward, so that he would be more than twenty miles west of Toulon. With this favouring wind, however, the *Blanche* should sight Lord Nelson's ships before noon. He wondered where the frigate was by this time. Probably she had headed out to sea again as soon as her investigation of the coast was finished, and might have passed quite close to the brig during the night. Captain Sainsbury would certainly not linger close inshore, for it was rumoured that the 60-gun French warship *Vengeur*, risking contact with a British line-of-battle ship in her anxiety to meet and fight the raiding frigate, had come out of Port Vendres harbour and was at sea.

He was on the point of leaving the cabin to give the helmsman the new course when the sound of running feet and excited voices on deck made him hurry up the ladder to the poop. In the grey light of dawn everything was grey – the wet decks, the figures of the seamen, the mist that enclosed a circle of heaving grey sea and cut down visibility to a hundred yards or less. Beamish met him as he emerged on deck.

'Frith's at the masthead, sir,' he said rapidly. 'Says he can see above the mist – there's a big vessel heading straight for us, about a mile away. Frith can only see the upper part of her masts – three of 'em, sir – but he swears she's French by her rig, and a warship.'

Septimus thought quickly. It might just be possible to dodge the strange vessel in the mist, but if he failed he must be ready with some other device. With six men and four small guns he could not hope to put up a fight against a big Frenchman. The wind had dropped still more and was from the south.

'Starboard your helm, Mr Beamish,' he said, 'and bring the wind astern.'

That would set the *Blanche* heading north again, but she would be creeping away from the Frenchman's course. If the enemy's lookout had not seen the brig's masts above the sea of mist, there was still a chance of getting away unseen. That chance could not be counted on, though.

'Wait!' he added as the big seaman turned to pass the order to the helmsman. 'Haul down our colours, Mr Beamish, and hoist the French flag. Have all arms concealed. If the Frenchman gets near enough to hail us, leave all the talking to me.'

'Aye aye, sir!' returned Beamish cheerfully, saluting and trotting aft.

Septimus, reflecting that a man who took emergencies with a broad grin, as Beamish did, was worth three men with worried expressions, hurried for'ard to where the rest of his men were swabbing the decks and setting to right the gear that had been disturbed by the gale. He selected Wallace, a slow-thinking Scot who could be relied upon to obey orders, and bade him get a musket and come below. To the rest he spoke briefly and with emphasis.

'If the Frenchman closes us, as he may do, we're a French brig. No man will speak a word while we're within earshot. Do you understand?'

'*Oui, oui,* sir,' answered O'Neill cheekily. 'But look now, Mr Quinn, sir,' he added hastily, 'I've a word or so of the Frenchy lingo, and I know a song in French, so I do.'

He began to sing a rowdy French drinking-song in a very passable tenor. Septimus repressed a smile.

'That'll do,' he said. 'You can sing that the moment we sight the Frenchman. No one else will utter a sound. In a moment I'll have you looking more like Frogs.'

He hastened below with Wallace at his heels. At the locked door of the forecastle he halted and made the seaman cock and present his musket. Then he unlocked the door and threw it wide, so that the prisoners could see the weapon levelled at them.

'*Attendez!*' he said sharply as the ten Frenchmen inside began to talk all at the same time. 'This musket is loaded. Every man here who has a cap will throw it at my feet – quickly!'

After a short hesitation, seven knitted woollen caps of various bright colours, the typical headgear of the French sailor in the Mediterranean, were flung on the deck in front of him. Septimus pointed a finger at one of the smaller men.

'You, there! Take off your jersey and give it to me!'

With much grumbling the little man obeyed.

'This seaman will remain outside the door to shoot any of you who make a noise,' warned the midshipman as, having picked up the garments, he locked the door again.

Before returning on deck he repeated his order in English for Wallace's benefit and then took off his blue uniform coat and pulled on the jersey. It was striped red and white and smelled of fish, but it would serve. As he came up the companionway Frith, a lean grim-faced seaman, was just sliding down the stay of the mainmast.

'I didn't want to hail the deck, sir,' he explained when Septimus demanded why he had left his post. 'The Frenchman's near enough to hear a hail. She's turned northerly – I'm pretty sure she's got a lookout and he's seen our mastheads.'

'Very good,' nodded the midshipman. 'Take these for'ard and see that every man wears one.' He gave Frith four of the woollen caps. 'And tell the fools to stow that noise!' he added as a burst of laughter came to his ears. 'We may dodge the Frogs yet if they keep quiet!'

Frith ran for'ard and Septimus, ramming a red woollen cap on his head, hurried to the poop. Beamish's eyes opened wide when he saw his young senior officer attired in a striped jersey and cap.

'It's ten to one they've seen us,' explained Septimus in a low voice. He gave one of the remaining caps to the helmsman – Dobbs – and the other to Beamish. 'Any moment now they may come out of the mist. When they do, wave your hand as if you know someone on board.'

'Aye aye, sir,' responded Beamish, trying to fit a very small sky-blue cap on to his massive head. 'But – beg pardon, sir, but you've got your spectacles on.'

Septimus, who had forgotten to remove them when he hurried up from the cabin, decided that they would add to his disguise and left them in place. He always felt more confident in an emergency with the familiar things resting on the bridge of his nose.

And now there was nothing to do but wait. The brig rolled very slowly through the oily grey waves, the circle of mist moving with her, as it seemed. The eyes of all on deck were on the wall of vapour on her larboard beam, for if the French vessel had seen the *Blanche* she must presently emerge through that grey curtain. Minutes that seemed like hours went by. Septimus, pacing the poop with his hands clasped behind him, had time to reflect upon their dangerous position. If the French warship found them, and their deception was detected, they could at best expect to inhabit a French prison for a very long time. He looked up at the tricolour flag flapping at the yardarm. It was considered legitimate in sea warfare to sail under false colours, so long as a vessel's true colours were hoisted before she began aggressive action. There was nothing unsporting about his attempt to save his command by that method.

He glanced at Beamish and nearly chuckled out loud. The huge seaman, with the tiny cap balanced absurdly on his mop of two-coloured hair, looked very unlike a Frenchman. Then he remembered his own appearance and chuckled in earnest. With his small figure enveloped in a striped jersey and a vivid red cap nodding its tassel above his spectacled face, he probably looked more like a monkey than anything else.

It was just as this thought crossed his mind that his eye was caught by a reddish appearance of the mist half-a-cable's length away on the larboard beam. In another moment the red-brown side of a big vessel broke through the mist. A broad black line ran along her flank, and in it fourteen gun-ports yawned threateningly, with fourteen more ranged above them in the bulwarks of the upper deck. Two stern-chasers and two carronades – she could be none other than the 60-gun *Vengeur*.

The French battleship sheered closer, her three great masts, carrying shortened sail, towering high above the brig. Septimus wished heartily that Charles Barry were with him, for Charles could speak fluent French. As it was, he could only hope that his bad accent would be taken for one of the various Provençal dialects, and confine himself to as few words as possible.

The expected hail floated clearly across the intervening space of water.

'What vessel's that? Answer immediately or I'll blow you out of the water!'

The French words were emphasised by a highly unpleasant oath. Evidently the captain of the *Vengeur* had no use for courtesy. Septimus cupped his hands to shout back. Behind him Beamish was waving cheerily to the figures clustered along the French vessel's rail, and from for'ard came O'Neill's high tenor voice singing his French drinking-song. It must be pretty convincing, after all. Septimus shouted with confidence.

"Brig *Blanche,* of Quelles. Captain Terray.'

'Whither bound?'

'Marseilles, with—' Septimus, unable to remember the French for 'vegetables', paused for a second. '*Cabages*,' he ended.

There was a pause. Then another hail, sounding more friendly. It's wording brought a sigh of relief from the midshipman, for it showed that his statements had been accepted.

'Have you see a British frigate?'

'*Non!*' returned Septimus, shrugging and spreading his shoulders. '*Rien du tout!*'

It was as much as he could do to keep from cheering. Another few seconds, and the *Vengeur* would have disappeared into the mist and the *Blanche* could resume her journey to Toulon.

And then the tables were turned in a moment. He heard a crash of glass, a girl's voice screaming something in rapid French. It was Jeanne. He had forgotten all about her. She had broken the stern-cabin window and given the game away.

The voice from the *Vengeur* hailed again, this time excited and savagely threatening.

'Heave-to instantly!'

To add point to the command, a cannon thundered and its ball whizzed over the *Blanche*'s bows. Midshipman Quinn looked at Seaman Tod Beamish.

'Bring her to, Mr Beamish,' he said softly.

'Aye aye, sir,' muttered Beamish. And then – 'Hard luck sir!'

4

Within ten minutes of that surrender, Mr Quinn and his six men were standing on the quarterdeck of the *Vengeur* with a dozen muskets covering them and the thin sallow face of the French captain grinning triumphantly at them.

He was a tall lean fellow, this Frenchman, with eyes that glinted fiercely as they gloated over his prisoners.

'*Sacrés Anglais!*' he spat. 'Insolents! Your impudence in sailing under the flag of France shall be repaid here and now. Pirates and ravagers! String them up by the neck, every cursed pirate of them – the spectacled boy first!'

His raised arm pointed to the *Vengeur's* yardarm. A slim figure ducked under his gold-laced sleeve and Jeanne Terray turned to confront him.

'M. le Capitaine Gruvel!' she cried, her eyes flashing. 'This is unworthy of you and of France! These are English seamen of the frigate *Althea*, and their midshipman is an officer of the English King's navy!'

'Be silent, mademoiselle!' he snarled at her. 'What is that to me?'

'To you it may be nothing,' she said contemptuously, 'though I should have thought your honour would mean something. To me it means that these men must be treated as prisoners of war. They used me fairly and courteously. I ask you now—'

'Stand aside, mademoiselle!' Gruvel waved her away. 'I command here, and I say they shall hang!' And he added a string of oaths.

Septimus, who had resumed his uniform and cocked hat and still wore his spectacles, understood enough of the captain's language to be seriously annoyed.

'Monsieur Gruvel,' he began, seeking for the correct French.

'Silence, pirate!' the man flung at him. 'Who bade you speak?'

'You did,' retorted Septimus severely, 'when you used such language before a lady. You are not a gentleman, sir.'

Captain Gruvel, thus insulted on his own quarterdeck, drew back his hand to strike. Then, feeling no doubt that his watching officers would lose respect for him if he struck a prisoner, he flung both arms wide.

'They shall all hang!' he vociferated. 'I take the responsibility!'

'You will – and your officers also, when I report your action to the naval authorities at Marseilles, Captain Gruvel!'

Jeanne Terray had pitched her clear voice to reach the ears of all. Septimus saw the anxious faces among the *Vengeur*'s officers, and heard their uneasy murmuring. Captain Gruvel heard it too. He glared at Jeanne, fingering his moustache. Then he swung round angrily to glower at Septimus.

'I have decided to spare you, pirate, since Madame le Capitaine here begs your lives! When you are in the prison at Marseilles you will wish you had been hanged, I promise you! Take them below!'

French marines closed round the *Althea*'s men, shepherding them with musket-butts. As Midshipman Quinn passed close to Jeanne Terray, he spoke rapidly from the corner of his mouth, in English.

'That was generous of you, mademoiselle.'

Without moving a muscle of her face, Jeanne replied, also in English.

'That was a very nice omelette, Monsieur Midshipman!' she said.

Chapter Seven

Mr Quinn's Troupe

I

The prison of La Ferronnerie in Marseilles was a sombre building of dark-grey stone standing like a huge square box just behind the bustle of the long quays of the port. A busy street ran in front of the prison's high wall, and the buildings opposite it cut off all view of the sea from the narrow barred window on the first floor where Midshipman Septimus Quinn was looking out. It was the afternoon of the day following the *Vengeur*'s capture of the midshipman and his six seamen. They had been in the prison of La Ferronnerie for nearly twenty-four hours, and already they had had enough of it.

The *Vengeur* had made all speed into Marseilles, the nearest port, with her prisoners. Their landing had been an unpleasant business, for the inhabitants of Marseilles gathered in crowds to fling oaths and stones at the seven British sailors as they were marched from the quays to the prison. It was well known along the southern coast of Napoleon Bonaparte's land that the frigate *Althea* had not only made many impudent raids along that coast but had also reduced Fort Flambeau, only five miles from Marseilles itself, to ruin. The frigate's men were not likely to be popular.

Midshipman Quinn, from his iron-barred window, could see the fronts of some warehouses and a narrow street below them where people – fishermen, market-women, and traders – went to and fro in the fitful sunlight of a cloudy September afternoon. On the blank wall of one of the warehouses was a gaudy poster announcing that 'THE GREAT ENRICO AND HIS TROUPE OF ACROBATS AND TUMBLERS' would visit Marseilles for the Carnival. Above the rooftops, where lines of washing were hanging, he could just make out the distant spars of ships at the quays. That was all.

He turned to look at the single room of their prison. Though it was merely four stone walls with a door in one and a window in another, it was less uncomfortable than he had expected. The Governor of La Ferronnerie had been a naval officer of France under the old régime, and Septimus suspected he was no true son of the New Republic, for he had treated his English prisoners well. They had straw for bedding, and their food, though consisting mainly of very thin soup and bread, was eatable. All the same, they were seven men accustomed to the freedom of the sea life and now cooped up together in one small bare room, and at the back of all their minds was one thought: *Escape.*

The midshipman cast a glance at each man in turn. Tod Beamish, the gigantic seaman whom he had made his second in command, was chatting gravely with Frith, the lean and grim-visaged Northumbrian. The fiery red head of O'Neill the Irishman could be seen in the gloom close to the pigtailed and whiskered face of Dobbs and the perky countenance of Eccles, the little Cockney. Wallace, the slow-moving Scot, was asleep on the straw, his snores undisturbed by the laughter O'Neill was provoking with his stories. They were a good half-dozen, as good as any he could have picked from the lower deck of a line-of-battle ship. Every one of them – even the unruly Dobbs – could be trusted to do his part in any attempt at escape. But how was that attempt to be made? Not by the window, which was closely barred with new iron and in full view of the street. There was a thirty-foot drop to a narrow yard and then iron-spiked railings on top of a high wall. That meant escaping by the door – through the interior of the prison, a hopeless task, apparently.

Beamish and Frith stopped their talk and approached him.

'Begging pardon, sir,' Beamish said, 'me and Frith's been talking of escape.'

'And I've been thinking of it,' nodded Septimus. 'Pray continue, Beamish.'

'Well, sir, it looks as if they'll bring us food twice a day. There's a guard with a musket who keeps his gun levelled from the doorway while his pal carries in the soup and bread. When they did it this forenoon the man with the gun was a fellow near as big as me.'

'Well?' said the midshipman as he paused. The others, including Wallace, who had been awakened by the sound of the magic word 'escape', were gathering round.

'The musket's the trouble, sir,' said Beamish, 'but Frith's suggested a way of getting over it. We all draw lots – all the seamen, sir – and the man as the lot falls to, he has to draw the fire of the musket. The rest of us overpower both the guards. Then I put on the uniform of the big guard, sir, and march all of you out of the prison.'

There was a chorus of agreement. The idea of a gamble whereby one of them lost his life to give the rest a chance of escape appealed to their sporting sense. Septimus regarded the big seaman thoughtfully.

'There's the germ of a good plan there, Beamish,' he said, 'but there are three things wrong with it. First, one of us is bound to be killed.'

'Never mind that, sir!' they broke in cheerfully. 'We'll take our chance, so we will!'

'No doubt,' said their youthful leader. 'But pipe down and attend to me. Second, the noise of the musket will alarm all the other guards, and there are at least ten in this prison. Beamish wouldn't have got the guard's trousers on before they'd be rushing up here. And third, there's the main door of this prison to pass afterwards, with an armed man always on duty there.'

No one spoke in reply to this unanswerable argument.

'Our aim, of course,' continued Septimus, 'would be to get to the quays and steal a boat. But even if we got outside the prison, with Beamish escorting us in his French uniform, we'd have little chance of getting to the shipping without being stopped and questioned. And none of us – least of all Beamish – can act the Frenchman well enough to deceive any native of this town.'

There was a pause. The attitudes of the seamen showed their disappointment.

'What'll we do, then, sir?' growled Dobbs at last. 'Ain't we to make a try at all?'

'We'll try, Dobbs – but we need to think out two more things yet. We want a way of dealing with the two men silently, and we want a disguise of some kind. For, as you know, the door of this room is too solid to break through and it's never opened during hours of darkness.'

He was sorry to pour cold water on their enthusiasm, but he had learned that British seamen, though brave as lions when they had fighting to do, were no good at strategy. He turned to look out of the window again, conscious that the men were discouraged. His eye fell on the gaudy poster advertising the visit of Enrico's 'Troupe', and it gave him an idea. He swung round with a smile.

'One thing we've to do, men,' he cried, 'is to keep ourselves in trim for when the chance comes. Physical exercises! Stand by, all – we'll show the Frogs a prison doesn't worry us. Leap-frog! Come on, Beamish – lead the line!'

He bent down, hands clasping ankles to 'make a back'. Beamish, looking far from enthusiastic, trotted up and vaulted over him.

'Look lively, there!' he growled at the others, and they followed with obvious reluctance.

It chanced that the little Cockney, Eccles, was next in line, and it was only natural that he should get stuck in trying to leap-frog over the huge Beamish. His yells and protests as the massive seaman shook him off like a bothersome fly started a laugh. And next moment, instead of behaving like a parcel of sulky infants, the men were shouting and skylarking in the highest spirits.

Leap-frog was quickly dropped in favour of feats of strength and balance. O'Neill displayed an astonishing expertness in turning 'cartwheels' and the solemn Frith unexpectedly walked twice round the room on his hands. Beamish seized the struggling Eccles and, placing his ham-like hand in the small of the little seaman's back, raised him at arm's length above his head and kept him there for some minutes. Dobbs and Wallace, not to be outdone, clutched each other round the waist and executed a wild dance, to the danger of the other performers in the confined space of their prison.

Septimus had no tricks of this kind, though he had once been able to juggle with three balls. He stood aside and laughed until his ribs ached at the antics of the seamen. At the height of the fun there came a thunderous knock on the door, and it flew open to reveal the prison guard with his musket levelled – the escort of their supper. The Frenchman's jaw dropped and he drew back a pace as he saw his prisoners apparently gone mad.

'*Entrez, mon ami*,' said Septimus encouragingly. 'This is the English way of cultivating an appetite.'

The guard scowled and watched them narrowly as his comrade brought in the tray with their soup and bread and set it on the floor inside the door. Then the door closed again and its massive iron lock clashed.

After their supper had been eaten the seamen seemed to lose their cheerfulness again. Sunset was past, their cell was darkening, and it was difficult to avoid thinking of their fate. For years they would be prisoners, for though 'exchanges' were frequently arranged for officers, captured French officers being released in exchange for British officers of equivalent rank, there was no such hope for a common seaman. They sat despondently on the straw or lay trying to sleep, while Septimus, watching the last light fade above Marseilles from his post by the window, cudgelled his brains for some plan of escape that would not be entirely hopeless. He could see none.

Their prison room was on the first floor of the building, and (as he remembered from their arrival) a short passage led from the door to the head of some stairs. That door had been thoroughly investigated by the prisoners. It was of solid oak five inches thick, with a new lock. Even Beamish's strength had no earthly chance of bursting it open, and they had no weapons or tools of any sort except the spoons – of pliable metal – which were used for eating their soup. The stairs led down into a stone-flagged hall where a sentry sat night and day close to the main entrance door of the building. Outside was a ten-foot-wide space all round the prison, beyond which was a wall twelve feet high topped by an iron fence of spikes. The big prison gate was in front of this wall, facing the Rue de la Ferronnerie, and a sentry was on duty there.

The outer wall was certainly unclimbable for one unaided man, Septimus reflected. But for two – or seven – men, one of whom was a giant like Tod Beamish, the passage of that barrier was not impossible. That was the only part of their escape route that seemed to offer any hope. To reach the wall, they had to overpower two guards, in silence; to deal with the sentry at the main door and unlock it with his keys; and to elude or overpower the sentry on the gate. And even if they did all this and got over the prison wall, they were seven Englishmen in naval rig in the midst of a great port crowded with their enemies. It all looked completely hopeless.

To fend off the despair that was creeping upon him he began to consider carefully each stage of the journey of escape. He found that he was unable to remember the position of the sentry at the prison gate, and called Beamish to him.

'Why, sir,' replied Beamish to his question, 'there's the sentry-box on the starboard hand as we came in through the gate – belay that, though. It was *outside* the gate, sir.'

That was something, Septimus told himself. Once in the courtyard within the wall, there was a good chance that the sentry on the other side of the massive oaken gate would not hear their further movements. That was one of their three obstacles gone.

'Still thinking of getting clear, sir?' said Beamish, who had been watching him eagerly. We're all with you, sir, no matter how desperate it seems.'

'Any plan I propose, Beamish, will have a fair chance of success,' returned the midshipman severely. 'It is our duty to rejoin our ship, not to indulge in desperate measures.'

'Aye aye, sir,' said Beamish, smothering a grin; he knew Septimus by this time. 'But – d'you think there's a bit of hope, sir?'

'Our only hope is in something occurring to help us, I'm afraid. We can do nothing at present, except turn in. There'll be no visitors for us tonight.'

But there Mr Quinn was mistaken. Half an hour later the door was flung open and two guards armed with muskets entered, followed by a third with a lantern. As the prisoners sat up blinking in the light a small elderly man dressed in black, with the tricolour of the Republic across his breast, came in carrying a large book, an inkhorn, and a pen.

'I am Jacques Rebuffat, clerk to the Governor,' he announced in excellent English. 'I require the full name of each prisoner. Those who can write will write them in this book themselves.'

The process of name-taking began. Septimus was left until last. When the clerk presented the open book for him to write in he saw the man's forefinger was holding to the page a slip of paper bearing two sentences in small handwriting. He read them quickly.

Omelette. He who shows this is my uncle, and can be trusted. Write how I may help you.

That was all, but the first word gave him the clue to its writer. Jeanne Terray, who had shown her friendship on board the *Vengeur*, was risking a great deal in sending that note. His impulse was to take no advantage of it, but a moment's thought showed him that his duty was to make use of her offer. There was very little time for planning, and if the germ of a plan had not been in his mind already he could not have seized this opportunity.

Pretending to have some difficulty in making the pen write, he contrived to write – in addition to his name in the book – a line on the slip of paper:

Please send our laundry, Bale Seventeen, and receive my thanks.

Monsieur Rebuffat closed the book as he finished writing. His face gave no sign that he had seen Septimus's message. He was turning to go when the midshipman remembered something.

'Pray inform me, monsieur,' he said quickly, 'whether we unfortunates will be able to see anything of the carnival from our prison window when it takes place – is it next week or this?'

'It takes place tomorrow,' the clerk replied coldly. 'And since it is a water carnival you English rascals will see nothing of it from your window. Guard, I have finished here. Precede me.'

The heavy door closed behind them, leaving the prisoners in darkness. But there was a gleam of hope in Midshipman Quinn's mind now. Jeanne's uncle, Jacques Rebuffat, had been careful to show no favour to the Englishmen, but he had taken the message and he had told Septimus two useful things. The carnival was tomorrow, and it was a water carnival – that meant it would be held on the waters of the harbour or on the quays.

If Jeanne Terray was as quick-witted as he thought her, she would know that 'Bale Seventeen' referred to a certain bale from the cargo of her brig *Blanche*. With the contents of that bale in his hands, Mr Quinn told himself, he and his men would have a chance – a very small chance – of escape.

2

Septimus told nothing of his plan to the six seamen that night. It might prove impossible for Jeanne to smuggle Bale Seventeen to them by the method he had suggested in his message, and he did not want to raise their hopes. But while they snored on the straw that night the midshipman was wakeful, planning all the details of an attempt at escape which depended on the arrival of their 'laundry' next day. He also spent some time in wondering what had caused Jeanne Terray to endeavour to help them. Doubtless the rudeness of the *Vengeur*'s captain, and his own polite treatment of the girl when she was his prisoner, had something to do with it, but he concluded that she must be secretly a Royalist and against Napoleon's rule.

Towards morning he snatched a little sleep but at first light he was peering out of the window of the prison. By getting his face close to the right-hand bars he could see down to the left. As he had thought, their first-floor room was at the corner of the building, and down below he could see the corner of the twelve-foot wall with its hedge of spikes. Beyond that corner was a space between it and the blank face of a building. There was evidently a narrow alley running along that side of the prison wall, and the space was its entrance from the Rue de la Ferronnerie. There was almost sure to be a way round the back of the prison building. Another small section of his plan dropped into place.

When the bang on the door announced the arrival of their meagre breakfast, he looked up eagerly. But there was no large parcel – only the usual bread and oatmeal broth. When this had been eaten, Septimus gave the men his first hint that there was a possibility of action.

'You may not know it,' he told them, 'but when we arrived in this prison we demanded that some of our clothing should be washed. If it comes back during the day, show no surprise.'

He would say nothing more, despite their pleas. Young as he was, he had learned that these seamen were very like children – easily depressed by disappointment. The plan must wait until he knew that its materials were to hand.

The hours passed. Outside the prison it was a brilliant day, and distant sounds of music and shouting told that the water carnival was in progress. The afternoon was half gone when they heard outside their door the voice of their guard protesting and an angry female voice answering.

'But see here, madame,' came the guard's growling tones, 'I saw no laundry go out from here! Show me what's in that bundle!'

'What do I care if you saw nothing, blind bat?' shouted the woman. 'It's the laundry for Room Six – and here's the Governor's clerk's signed pass stuck on it! Isn't that good enough for you?'

'Oh, all right then!' Septimus, listening eagerly, gasped with relief as he heard that. 'Heave it into the room and get out, vixen!'

The door opened, showing the usual threatening musket, and a bundle wrapped in an old tablecloth was thrown in.

'Maybe you dirty English will smell a bit sweeter now!' snarled the guard, and the door clanged shut again.

Septimus gestured to the seamen to be silent until the footsteps of the guard and the laundress had echoed away down the passage. Then he untied the bundle. Inside it was the bale – Bale Seventeen – which he had seen listed on the *Blanche*'s papers as 'Theatrical Costumes for Marseilles'. Five minutes later, with the six men clustered round him and listening eagerly, he was outlining his plan of escape. And the rest of that afternoon was spent in rehearsing the first part of the plan and ensuring that every man knew his part.

The prisoners' supper was usually brought at sunset, but on this day – perhaps because the off-duty guards wished to go to the carnival – the thunderous knock on the door came half an hour earlier than usual. The two guards had an invariable system to guard against any attack on them by the prisoners. The door of the prisoners' room opened outwards, so there was no possibility of anyone hiding behind the door to surprise and overcome a guard. Thus, the door was first pulled open to reveal a guard with musket cocked and presented, standing just outside the door. Then the second guard would enter carrying the tray of food while the musket-muzzle swung to cover any prisoner who made a suspicious movement. Midshipman Quinn's plan had to make the most of this situation. It had to seize the first half-second of time when the door opened, and it had to divert the attention of the man with the musket immediately.

So, when the supper-time banging on the door was followed by the flinging open of the door, the armed guard was astounded at the sight before him. A gigantic lady some nine feet high, in bonnet and gown, was standing in the centre of the room. It was Septimus Quinn seated on the shoulders of Tod Beamish, whose body was hidden by an ingenious arrangement of female garments, but the guard was not to know that. He was not to know much more, in fact. For, profiting by that moment of incredulous astonishment, two of the five men who had been flattened against the wall inside the door sprang upon him. Simultaneously the other three darted past him and dealt with his comrade.

Every movement of this had been practised over and over again and it was all done in a very few seconds. Frith brought the edge of his granite-hard hand in a chopping blow to the base of the armed guard's skull while Dobbs wrested the musket from him in one savage snatch. The man collapsed with no more than a groan and Frith caught him as he fell. Meanwhile, O'Neill had stifled the second guard's yell in the nick of time and held him while Wallace's heavy fist stunned him, the tray of food being neatly caught by Eccles and saved from crashing to the floor. In six seconds from the moment the door had opened it was being gently closed again and deft hands were already at work gagging and binding the unconscious guards with strips made from the 'theatrical costumes'. The first part of the plan had succeeded completely.

What sort of theatrical entertainment those costumes were intended for, Septimus never discovered. There were women's dresses of some mediaeval period, men's doublets and hose of patched but brightly-coloured material, a leopard-skin, a Court dress of black satin – knee-breeches and silver-buttoned coat – one or two wigs and moustaches, and various paints in small boxes. He had already made a selection of these and allocated to each man a costume. While the captured guards were being secured he was listening at the crack of the door for any sign of an alarm being raised. There was none. He ordered his men into their costumes at once.

There was a good deal of smothered laughter as they dressed. Beamish, in tights and a leopard skin, made an impressive Strong Man. Little Eccles and lumpish Wallace were transformed, with the aid of wigs and gowns, into two highly-painted ladies, while O'Neill and Frith, in doublets and hose with pointed hats above their newly-moustached faces, looked like a pair of lean outlaws from Sherwood Forest. Dobbs, with a false black beard and a motley costume of ribbons and bows, declared himself to be the Wild Man from Timbuctoo. As for Septimus, he had arrayed himself in the black Court costume and a dark moustache and imperial, adding to this his spectacles to give him confidence and disguise him still more. He had contrived three rough balls out of tightly-bound linen and had been practising his juggling act with them.

When the men were all ready he gathered them round him for a final instruction. They munched bread as they listened, for there was no knowing where their next meal would come from.

'You are my Troupe,' he told them, 'and I am the Great Enrico. Your order when we get into the streets – if we get that far – you know. You'll follow me closely and no man of you will speak a word of English – you can yell as much as you like. But before that there must be absolute silence until I give the word. You understand?'

'Aye aye, sir!'

'Then we'll up anchor at once. Beamish, Dobbs, Frith – follow me in that order.'

He opened the door cautiously. Apart from the muffled sound of voices in other rooms of the prison, all was quiet. When they were all out of the room he locked the door and dropped the key into his pocket. Then, moving swiftly and silently in single file, they tiptoed along the passage to the head of the stairs. Here they halted while Septimus bent to peer down into the stone-flagged hall below. He could just see the table which stood on the right of the heavy main door, and a man in the uniform of the prison guards lounging in a chair at the table. His face was turned towards the stairs, and for an instant Septimus thought he had seen the group in the shadows at the stairhead. But the guard continued his occupation of picking his teeth and the midshipman withdrew silently to consider the next move.

They could not start down the stairs without being seen by the guard. There was a pistol on the table in front of the man, and three muskets stood in a rack within arm's length of him. What was more, he could probably bring other guards into the hall by raising his voice. Was this, after all, to be the end of their attempt?

Septimus felt the hard shape of the key in his pocket, and an idea occurred to him. It was a simple one and might fail, but it was their only chance so far as he could see. He held one finger aloft – the agreed sign to his followers to be ready for instant action – and then, bending down until he was crouching on the top stair, he threw the key through the bannisters so that it fell with a clang into a corner of the hall.

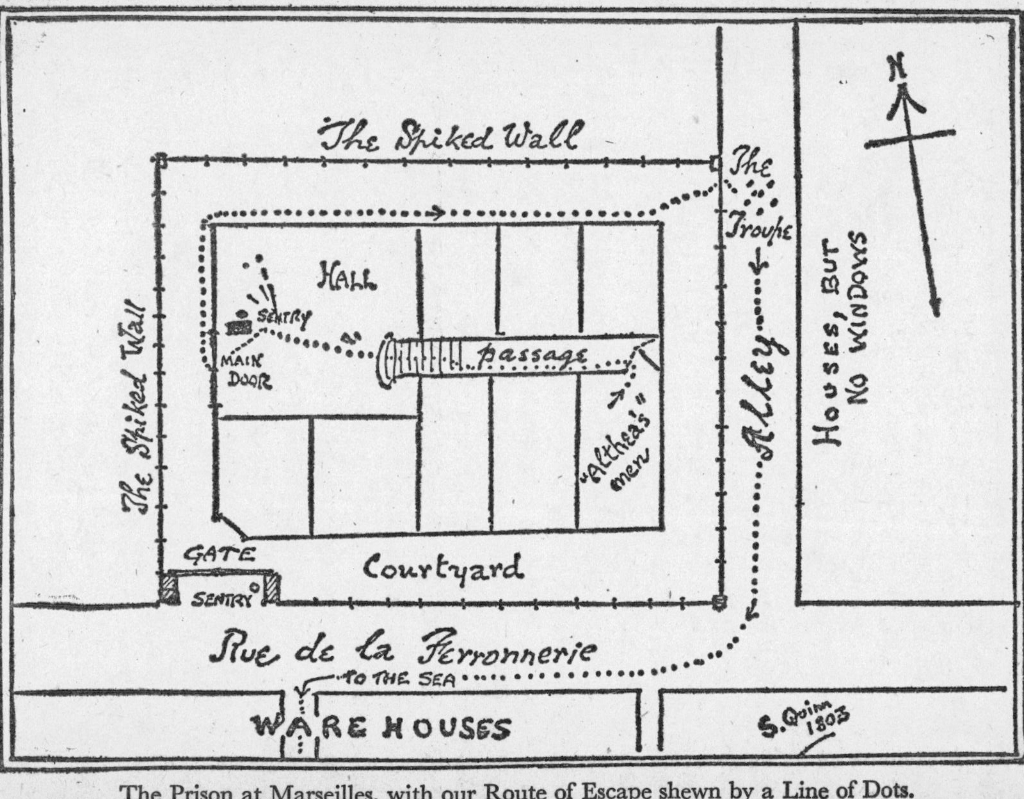

The Prison at Marseilles, with our Route of Escape shewn by a Line of Dots.
A Sketch Plan from the private Log of Midshipman Quinn.

The guard at the table stopped picking his teeth and stood up, peering not up the stairs but into that corner. It was a gloomy hall and he decided – as Septimus had hoped – to investigate the noise. The midshipman waited until he was halfway across the hall and then sped noiselessly down the stairs with his men at his heels.

The guard heard them before they were upon him, but he had no time for more than a surprised grunt before Dobbs's enormous hand was clamped over his mouth. The fist of Tod Beamish descended once upon his skull, and that was enough. They laid the unconscious man in the shadows and Septimus, who had gone straight to the board above the table where keys were hanging on hooks, beckoned them to him. The third key he tried was the right one. The main door swung slowly open – creaking so loudly that it sounded like a voice shrieking that they were escaping – and Septimus peered cautiously out.

He looked first to the left. Fifty paces away along the cobbled yard was the main gate of the prison. It was closed, of course, and its massive bulk prevented anyone passing along the Rue de la Ferronnerie from seeing into the courtyard. To the right the cobbled way, with the tall spiked wall rising on its left and the wall of the prison on its other side, ran to a right-angled corner. There was no one in sight. Septimus beckoned to his oddly-clad party and they slipped out through the door.

Not a moment could be wasted, for the discovery of the unconscious guard in the hall might be made at any time. In silence, but trotting fast, they rounded the corner and hurried along the back of the building to its next corner. Opposite them now rose the wall beyond which was the alley running down to the main street. That twelve-foot barrier of smooth masonry, with its crowning fringe of iron spikes, was all that stood between them and the streets where men moved freely. They went to work at once, and still in silence, for all this had been practised in their prison that afternoon.

Frith stood close to the wall and facing it, supporting himself against it with bent arms. He was nearly as tall as Beamish but lean where the other was broad, and his wiry frame shook as the huge seaman mounted to stand on his shoulders. With his hands hooked round the base of the iron spikes, Beamish kicked off so strongly that Frith staggered and almost collapsed, but the 'Strong Man' was up and clinging to the spikes with his feet braced against the wall. In a second he was back again – Frith recovering just in time to receive him – crouching on his shipmate's shoulders with a finger to his lips enjoining silence. The footsteps and voices of two men, approaching along the alley and then passing away again, explained his action. When they had gone he hauled himself up once again and, after a swift glance right and left, signalled the coast clear.

Dobbs was already making a 'ladder' for Frith, who sprang up to hang from the fence of spikes with one foot braced on the wall-top four feet away from where Beamish was doing the same. Septimus, mounting on Dobbs's broad shoulders, could reach and grasp the hands the men above reached down to him. He swung up like a feather and was soon straddling carefully over the spikes and lowering himself until he hung from their bases with his legs dangling down the outside of the wall. When he let go, the drop seemed a big one although it was only six feet. But he landed with no worse injury than two smarting soles. One by one the rest came over until only Dobbs was left. Beamish lowered himself until Dobbs could grasp his leg, and with a grunt and a struggle the last man was up.

Until they were all down on the cobbles of the alley, Midshipman Quinn passed some very trying moments. The alley was not a frequented one, luckily, and no one came down it or entered it from the bottom end. But the Rue de la Ferronnerie ran across that bottom end, distant only about seventy yards, and three people passed the narrow opening while the crossing of the wall was taking place. If one of those three passers-by had glanced up the alley as he passed, the game would have been up. But they did not.

'Oo! 'Ug me tight, dearie!' squeaked the irrepressible Eccles in falsetto tones as he made the descent. And Septimus, turning sharply to reprimand him, had to grin instead when he saw the little Cockney's smirking face in its imitation curls, and his languishing leer as he pretended to collapse into Beamish's arms.

'Form, now!' he snapped. 'Look lively! Smile, every man – and make plenty of noise when we reach the street yonder. Ready? Then forward!'

A few minutes later those citizens of Marseilles who chanced to be passing along the Rue de la Ferronnerie halted to stare, and stood still to laugh and applaud, as a procession of seven persons swung into the street from a side road.

First came a small and dapper gentleman in a black Court dress, his spectacled face adorned with moustache and small pointed beard, juggling with three balls and bowing right and left as he juggled. On either side and a little behind him were two lithe men in red-and-green suits, like foresters, one of whom appeared to prefer walking on his hands to progressing like ordinary folk, while the other was a Catherine Wheel of coloured legs and arms as he flung himself along in a series of cart-wheels, emitting joyful shouts as he did so. Next came a gigantic man whose swelling muscles were revealed by the folds of a leopard-skin worn over one shoulder. Held aloft on the palm of one hand he supported what appeared to be a girl in flowing draperies, a girl with remarkably golden locks who kissed her bony fingers to the citizens. Lastly, and causing peals of laughter from the onlookers, there came a portly girl in red ringlets and a vivid yellow gown (the lumbering Wallace) and a hairy ape-like creature decked in ribbons and bows. It is to be feared that if Mr Septimus Quinn could have seen the antics of Dobbs and Wallace, he would have thought them extremely vulgar; but the citizens of Marseilles seemed to find them funny in the extreme.

One or two flags and streamers were the only signs of carnival in the Rue de la Ferronnerie, but from the direction of the quays came the sounds of revelry – a band was playing, and people were singing and shouting. Septimus had turned to the right when he led his motley crew out of the alley. He now took the first turning on the left, making towards the sea-front, while French men and women waved and shouted jests at him.

The sky overhead was red with sunset, and a little breeze bore the smell of salt to their nostrils. A new wildness came into the antics of Mr Quinn's Troupe. They were free, and somewhere close at hand was their road of escape, their familiar friend, their home – the sea.

3

The French Republic's sloop-of-war *Chasseur* lay at her moorings well out in the big harbour of Marseilles. She was a slim and speedy little craft and had been a smuggler before the naval authorities had given her six twelve-pounders and a naval crew – only to find that there was little work for her to do. The French fleet was penned in Toulon harbour, and except for a few warships that made hasty ventures out of port and back again no French vessels put to sea. There was always the danger of meeting one of the squadrons of the hated Nelson, or a roving frigate like the *Althea* which had been doing such damage along the coast. The *Chasseur* made a sally out of Marseilles once a week, for exercise, and that was all.

On this evening of 28th September, the night of the Marseilles water carnival, the sloop was a graceful black outline on the many-coloured waters of the harbour. The fading crimson of sunset was outdone by the brilliant lights along the waterfront, where torchlight processions and fireworks were already beginning, their flares and trails of light reflected on the slow-moving surface.

'A pretty picture, *pardieu*!' remarked Lieutenant-de-Vaisseau Brunel as he leaned on the sloop's after-rail. 'Don't you agree, Philippe?'

Sous-Officier Philippe Cartier grunted. 'It'd be prettier if we were somewhat nearer to it,' he said. '*Diable!* But I'd like to be dancing with a girl or draining my fifth glass in a café! Why did we have to be picked for duty aboard?'

'Someone has to keep the deck-watch on this ship,' retorted Brunel. 'For my part, I'd rather be on board the *Vengeur*. She sailed yesterday to hunt that impudent English frigate, and they may have come to grips by now.'

'*Vengeur* won't have much trouble with a mere frigate, if she catches her,' Cartier remarked. '*Diable!* I'm hungry. Who's on board, besides Lemaire?'

'No one. Captain Desmoulins gave leave to all the men except Cook Lemaire – and us.'

'A nice thing!' grumbled Cartier, making funnels of his hands the better to watch the movement on the quays. 'Everyone but us having fun on shore. I can see them dancing down by the water there – hear the music?'

He began to execute some dance steps on the deck. Brunel sighed as he too gazed at the galaxy of lights ashore.

'Some of the fishing-boats have coloured lanterns rigged in them,' he said. 'They're pulling about the harbour. Maybe one of them will come out here.'

Cartier stopped his dancing. '*Diable!* But that would be good fun!' he said eagerly. 'I suppose, Lieutenant, we couldn't invite them on board – just for a few minutes? We could have a little party – especially if there happened to be some presentable females with them!'

Brunel removed his cocked hat to scratch his head.

'Well, I don't know,' he said doubtfully. 'Captain Desmoulins left no instructions—'

'Bah to Captain Desmoulins!' broke in Cartier disrespectfully. 'By this time he's dead drunk in some café – you know him. And look! One of the illuminated boats is coming out in this direction. Shall I give her a hail – just for a joke?'

The Lieutenant-de-Vaisseau hesitated. He was as disgusted as Cartier at being left on board and deprived of an evening's revelry, but he was in temporary command of the *Chasseur,* and for a French naval officer of the Republic he was a dutiful young man.

'No,' he said at last. 'If the boat comes alongside, that's another matter. But no hailing her, Philippe.'

Both the young Frenchmen watched the approach of the lantern-hung boat with some excitement. She was a large open boat, with the gondola-like prow of the Mediterranean, and she was being pulled by oars. A string of gaily-painted lanterns was hung from stem to stern, and as she came nearer the sound of a man's voice singing a French drinking-song came pleasantly across the water to their ears.

'Nice voice that fellow's got,' commented Brunel. 'I once heard an Irish tenor sing, when I was in Dublin during the Peace, and this man has the same—'

'Lieutenant!' interrupted his companion excitedly. 'I can see women's dresses in that boat! There are some girls with them!'

'H'm!' grunted Brunel. 'If I remember aright, Lemaire can play the concertina. We *could* have half-an-hour's gaiety, perhaps – there's room for dancing on the deck here. But mind you, Sous-Officier Cartier – only half-an-hour. We might find ourselves bowing to Madame la Guillotine if we're found out!'

'I'll risk it,' laughed Cartier. 'See! The boat's making straight for us.'

On came the illuminated craft, a picturesque sight with all its lanterns reflected in the rippled black water. The singer certainly had a sweet voice, although he seemed to know only one song. The girls' dresses could be seen through the twilight now, and a high-pitched voice emitted a trill of laughter. A civilian boat, thought Brunel, must not be allowed to come nearer without being hailed.

'Boat, there!' he shouted. 'Who are you?'

The reply came in a confident tone but with a marked foreign accent.

'I am the Great Enrico, M. le Capitaine, and with me are the ladies and gentlemen of my troupe. May we bring you some of the gaiety of Carnival in the midst of your duties?'

'It's the Italian fellow,' whispered Cartier. 'I saw the notices – he has a troupe of acrobats and so on. I'll wager the girls are pretty. Let's have them on board, Lieutenant!'

'Monsieur Enrico!' called Brunel. 'Come alongside, if you please. There are only three of us on board, but we may find you some entertainment.'

'*Bon!*' came the reply, and Cartier, rubbing his hands gleefully, echoed it.

The lantern-hung boat glided up to the sloop's side. Brunel noted that the men at the oars appeared to be two of Enrico's troupe, as they were in fantastic costumes. But he thought no more about it, nor did he see the two boatmen lying unconscious under the thwarts. As for Cartier, he was staring at the wearers of the gaily-coloured dresses.

'I don't think much of the fat one,' he muttered in the Lieutenant's ear. 'She must be the Bearded Lady of the troupe. The little one looks all right, though.'

Brunel waved him aside impatiently. Later he was to wish he had paid more attention to Cartier's first remark. (Seaman Wallace, who had not shaved for five days, was indeed showing a very hairy cheek for a young lady.) The boat made fast, and a dapper gentleman in her bows looked up inquiringly at the two officers. In the yellow lantern-light they could see that he wore spectacles and a pointed moustache and beard, and was dressed in a black satin Court costume.

'May we come on board, M. le Capitaine?' he asked deferentially.

'Please do so,' replied Brunel, 'and bring your friends. Perhaps you'll pass up a lantern or two – we've not much light on deck here and it's getting dark.'

'Thank you, sir – certainly I will do so.'

'Dreadful accent the Italian fellow's got,' murmured Cartier. '*Diable,* Lieutenant!' he added. 'We'd better get some wine on deck. I'll call Lemaire, shall I?'

Without waiting for Brunel's reply he shouted the French sea-cook's name. Meanwhile, the Great Enrico and his Troupe were clambering on board. Their leader greeted Lieutenant Brunel with a great deal of bowing and graceful gesture, while a giant in a leopard skin, a golden-haired girl in white, a very broad girl in yellow, and three gaudily-attired men, swung themselves on board. Cartier was struck with the amazing ease with which the ladies of the troupe climbed to the deck – even the fat one he had named 'the Bearded Lady'. Two of the men had brought lanterns up from the boat, but the light showed very little of the newcomers' faces. Cartier bowed to the smaller of the two girls.

'Your humble servant, mademoiselle,' he said with a bold glance. 'Welcome to the warship *Chasseur*.'

The lady, who had a pert monkey-like face and heavily-rouged cheeks, narrowly escaped falling over as she attempted to curtsey. She made no reply except a high-pitched giggle, and rolled her eyes at him alarmingly. That was Seaman Eccles's idea of ladylike behaviour. Before Cartier could continue this interesting conversation the French seaman Lemaire came hurrying aft along the shadowy deck. As he reached the Lieutenant he gasped at the sight of the strange figures, half-visible in the glimmer of light from the lanterns, that stood about the deck round his commanding officer.

'Monsieur Enrico and his friends will take wine, Lemaire. Bring up three bottles of the Bordeaux,' ordered Brunel.

'*Oui, M. le Lieutenant*,' stammered the man. His eyes were goggling at the huge man in leopard-skin, and he made no move to obey.

'Well, fool?' snapped Brunel. 'Are you asleep? Go!'

'*Oui, oui, monsieur*!' Lemaire turned hastily to obey.

'Do not go yet, Lemaire,' said a new voice sharply. 'My Strong Man wishes to speak to you.'

The Frenchman halted at the Great Enrico's words. The Strong Man stepped up to him and spoke in a strange tongue.

'By your leave, messmate!'

His clenched fist rose and fell. Lemaire, struck on the crown of the head, fell to the deck.

'What in the name of—'

Brunel had no chance to say more. Two of the gaudily-clad fellows had seized his arms while the Great Enrico clapped a hand tightly over his mouth. At the same time Cartier found himself in the far-from-loving embraces of the two 'ladies', and discovered that the hand of the Bearded Lady, which was pressed firmly upon the lower part of his face, was exceedingly hard and horny. In five minutes the three Frenchmen who had been left on board the *Chasseur* were lying gagged and bound in their bunks below decks and the sloop was in the hands of the Great Enrico and his Troupe.

It was Beamish who had seen the trim little vessel lying well out on the harbour waters as the Troupe gambolled its way among the merry-makers on the quays. He had muttered in his leader's ear that if they could get aboard that craft, they would have a fast sailer and a worthy prize. Septimus, after some rapid thought, had decided to take the chance. He had led his men to one of the many boats that plied for hire about the harbour and ordered the two boatmen, in a lordly manner, to pull out to the sloop, where – he asserted – they had been invited to perform before the captain.

It had been a simple matter to deal with the two boatmen. The moment the boat passed behind the hull of a fishing-vessel and was hidden from the quays, the oarsmen had been pulled over backwards and sat on, while two of the Troupe took their place. Luck had been with them on their arrival at the sloop, for the officer in charge had himself revealed that there were only three men on board.

Now came an even trickier part of the business. There was a light breeze, just sufficient to move the sloop out of harbour. But she would have to pass the entrance between two jetties or moles, each of which was certain to have cannons emplaced on it and men on watch. It would not do to risk being fired into from both sides.

Septimus cast a rapid glance all round his captured vessel. There was no other craft near her, and it was unlikely that anyone had seen, in the deepening twilight with its many sparkling lights, the neat disposal of her officers. Leaving Beamish to superintend the preparation of the mainsail and jib for hoisting, the midshipman selected Dobbs as having the most terrifying aspect of all his men, and took him below. Cartier had seemed the less reliable of the two French officers and it was to his cabin that he went with his henchman.

Cartier, lying trussed and gagged on his bunk, twitched with terror, as in the dim lantern-light, he saw the fierce-looking Dobbs – now without his feminine disguise – showing his teeth and flourishing a large knife filched from the galley. It was scarcely necessary for Septimus to point out, as he did, that unless Cartier helped them through the harbour entrance they might be fired into, and both Cartier and Brunel might be killed. Faced with the piratical Dobbs and his knife, Cartier hastily agreed to tell them what lights should be shown and to answer the hail of the harbour watch.

4

Moving ghost-like through the summer night, a small vessel with a graceful single mast and two sails set crept into the narrow passage which led out of Marseilles harbour. From the jibboom hung two lanterns, one above the other.

'What vessel's that?' came the hail from the mole on the starboard hand.

'*Chasseur* – Captain Desmoulins!'

'Whither bound?'

'On night manœuvres!'

'That's Sous-Officer Cartier speaking, sir,' said the sergeant of gunners to his officer.

'Pass, *Chasseur* – and good fortune to you!' shouted the officer, adding to his sergeant, 'Desmoulins is getting very dutiful – manœuvres on carnival night, *pardieu*!'

The sloop glided slowly out of the harbour entrance. Philippe Cartier, who had been speaking with some difficulty owing to the fact that the point of Seaman Dobbs's knife was pricking the back of his neck, was escorted below.

'Make sail, Mr Beamish, if you please,' ordered her new commander, no longer the Great Enrico but Mr Midshipman Septimus Quinn. 'And don't raise your voice,' he added. 'We're still within earshot of the moles.'

Forestaysail and gaff-topsail rose and bellied out in the light breeze, a girlish giggle from aloft indicating that Seaman Eccles was doing his part. The sloop *Chasseur* curtseyed to the wind and headed seaward, bound for Lord Nelson's fleet sixty miles away off Toulon.

Chapter Eight

The Sea Fight

I

Lieutenant-de-Vaisseau Charles Brunel writhed and twisted on his bunk, trying to rid himself of the constricting bonds that tied his hands and feet. It was his own bunk, in his own cabin in the French sloop-of-war *Chasseur*. That was the most galling thing of all. To be a prisoner on board his own ship, and because of his own carelessness, was a thing that made him hot with shame whenever he thought of it – and he had thought of it continuously during the twelve hours the sloop had been at sea. For she was at sea, manned by the impudent Englishmen who had captured her and taken her out of Marseilles harbour on the previous evening.

In the side of Brunel's bunk there was a projecting nail-head. It was very difficult to get the cord that bound his wrists against that tiny rim of sharp metal and he could only do it for a few minutes at a time, but he kept doggedly rubbing the cord against it. So far there was no sign that he was fraying the cord.

He paused for a while to ease his aching muscles. What a fool, a criminally careless fool, he had been! How the Englishmen had escaped from their prison and obtained the fantastic disguises in which they had come aboard, Brunel could not guess. The fact remained that he, Charles Brunel, had himself invited them on board, without orders from his absent captain and without troubling to make certain they were what they appeared to be. As he lay helpless in his bunk, with the sloop pitching rhythmically over the waves of the Mediterranean, he was both furious and ashamed.

He was also doggedly resolved to make amends for his folly – if ever he could get free.

He was about to begin again on his attempt to fray his bonds when the door of the cabin opened and a smallish young man – a mere boy, in fact – came in. Lieutenant Brunel, after a moment's staring, recognised the leader of the English seamen.

'Good morning, Lieutenant,' said the newcomer in slow but understandable French. 'I trust you are not too uncomfortable?'

Midshipman Septimus Quinn had removed the moustache and small beard which had disguised him as the Great Enrico, but was still wearing the black satin coat and knee-breeches. He was also wearing his spectacles, for he had just come from the captain's cabin where he had been working out the sloop's course for Toulon. As the French Lieutenant made no reply to his greeting, he sat down on the side of the bunk and looked sympathetically at his captured foe over the steel rims of his glasses.

'Permit me once again to point out, Monsieur Brunel,' he said, 'that if you would give me your parole – your word of honour to attempt no escape or other action against us – I could release you from those unpleasant bonds and you could walk about on deck instead of being cooped up here.'

'I will not give my parole,' Brunel said sullenly.

'The other officer, Monsieur Cartier, has given his parole,' Septimus pointed out. 'It would be greatly to your advantage, Lieutenant, if you also would—'

'I refuse!' broke in the other loudly.

The midshipman started to shrug his shoulders and checked himself quickly. This talking in French lingo made one use French gestures. He must guard against becoming too much like a Frog!

'Then you must remain as you are,' he said. 'Food will be brought to you and your hands untied so that you can eat it. Otherwise, you have only yourself to thank for your position.'

'Do I not know it?' Brunel broke out passionately. 'Was it not I myself who asked you and your cursed Troupe on board? Your Strong Man and your acrobats—'

'Not forgetting the charming ladies,' put in Mr Quinn with a chuckle. 'But I think I understand you, Lieutenant,' he added more seriously. 'You blame yourself and will take the consequences. Also, perhaps, you are hoping that we shall encounter the sixty-gun French warship *Vengeur*.'

Charles Brunel gave a start, and Septimus, who was watching him, noticed it.

'Yes, Monsieur Brunel,' he nodded. 'Sous-Officier Cartier has informed me that the *Vengeur* sailed from Marseilles thirty-six hours ago in search of His Majesty's frigate *Althea*, my own ship. So far nothing has been seen of her, and it's quite probable that the frigate has already reached Lord Nelson's fleet off Toulon. When this vessel also reaches the Toulon fleet, you will be honourably treated as a prisoner of war. I repeat, Monsieur, you have nothing to gain by refusing your parole.'

'Yet I still refuse it,' growled Brunel.

Septimus took off his spectacles, wiped them, and put them in his pocket.

'*Bien,* Lieutenant Brunel,' he said, 'I shall not ask you for it again. You may like to know that it is now two bells in the forenoon watch with a fair breeze blowing from due west, and that I hope to be with Lord Nelson's fleet by nightfall.' He stood up. 'It is warm in here – I'll send a glass of wine down to you.'

'I want no wine – you understand? No wine!'

Brunel spoke savagely, and writhed over until his face was turned to the cabin bulkhead. Septimus, after a moment's hesitation, bade him *au revoir* and went out of the cabin.

Left alone once more, Charles Brunel recommenced rubbing his bonds against the protruding nail-head. He had not been unmindful of his enemy's courtesy in offering him wine, but he had refused it because it meant that his hands might be untied. Whoever untied them might notice the fraying of the cord which he hoped had begun. If he could but free his hands it would be easy to free his ankles. And then? The sloop's powder-magazine was below decks amidships, and locked. He could not hope to break into it unobserved. But he might reach the store where the cotton-waste and oily rags were kept, and there was flint-and-steel there too. He could start a fire that a meagre crew of six English seamen would not readily put out, and that fire would eventually reach the magazine. There would be an end of Charles Brunel as well as of the Englishmen, but Brunel cared nothing for that. He was in the mood to give his life to wipe out the shame of his capture.

It was two bells in the forenoon watch, that spectacled youth had told him. At noon his food would be brought to him. They would untie his hands then and see the frayed cord. If he was to get free, he had only three hours – or less – to manage it. He set to work with furious energy, rubbing and rubbing at the fraying of the cord.

Midshipman Quinn made his way slowly on deck. He was inclined to like Lieutenant Brunel, and felt a certain sympathy for the Frenchman. However, if the young man chose to be sullen and discourteous he could do nothing about it. He came up into the sunshine of a bright and windy September morning, and his spirits rose as he remembered what he had achieved. Not only had he brought all his six men safely out of the clutches of the enemy – out of a French prison and a great French port – but he had also taken a valuable prize. If he could bring the *Chasseur* into the safety of the Toulon fleet he would have done a notable piece of work which would probably be reported in the *Gazette* and advance his chances of early promotion. And unless the sloop fell in with the *Vengeur* there was every reason that this would happen.

The sloop was bowling merrily along under full sail. Beamish had been right when he judged her a fast sailer. On every side stretched the brilliant blue, flecked with white, of the Mediterranean, for Mr Quinn was keeping the French coast below the horizon on his larboard hand. Fortunately a sloop-rigged vessel, with a single mast, a jib, mainsail, forestaysail and gaff-topsail, was not difficult to handle with a skeleton crew. But it took all six of his crew to put her about or shorten sail. Just now she was running free, and the trustworthy Frith at the helm needed no assistance. But every man, he noticed with pleasure, was on deck and busy.

O'Neill's red head could be discerned high above the deck where he was perched on the truck of the mast as lookout. Wallace and Eccles, their paint and feminine draperies removed, were squatting under the weather bulwarks constructing the British colours out of some strips of signal bunting – neither they nor Midshipman Quinn would feel happy until those colours could be hoisted on their prize. Dobbs and Beamish were bending over one of the six twelve-pounder guns the sloop carried, getting to know the slight differences between its elevating system and the system used on British sea cannon. Dobbs had been a gunlayer on board the *Althea,* and had already spent some hours that morning training his shipmates in running-out and laying the French guns. Like O'Neill and Frith, Seaman Dobbs still wore the motley costume of tights and ribbons in which he had made his escape. And as for the gigantic Beamish, he was still wearing the leopard-skin of the Strong Man. Only two of his men, reflected Septimus, looked like British seamen. He doubted whether so fantastic a crew had ever appeared on the deck of a warship, French or English.

After exchanging a word with Frith at the helm, the midshipman was about to walk for'ard and talk to Beamish when Sous-Officier Cartier, French prisoner on parole, crossed the deck to intercept him.

'A friendly wind for you, Monsieur Quinn,' he said with his ingratiating smile. 'I wish you good fortune in rejoining your own ship at an early date.'

'For the moment, Monsieur Cartier,' retorted Septimus, '*this* is my ship.'

He passed on, leaving Cartier to return with a shrug to his lounging-place by the lee rail. Septimus did not like Cartier, who showed himself too eager to make friends with his captors. He much preferred the sullen Brunel. Though Cartier had given his parole, and had readily answered all the questions put to him, the midshipman did not trust the man and had given orders to Dobbs to keep an unobtrusive eye on his movements.

Tod Beamish straightened himself and knuckled his forehead as Midshipman Quinn approached.

'Guns all ready, Mr Beamish?'

'Ready and trim, sir,' replied the big seaman, grinning as Septimus used the 'Mister' that indicated that Beamish was second-in-command – temporarily – of a warship. 'Me and Dobbs, we've got these here trunnions sorted out now. We'll not be able to fire a broadside of more 'n two guns, though, sir – not with a crew of six all told.'

'But the *Chasseur* can show a clean pair of heels to anything near her size,' nodded Septimus thoughtfully. 'Can she outpace the *Vengeur*, do you think?'

Beamish shook his thatch of tow-coloured hair. 'I doubt it, sir. That Monseer Cartier, he says *Vengeur*'s very fast for a ship-rigged vessel.'

'Then we'll fight for it if we meet her.' Mr Quinn looked his second-in-command in the eye. 'We've no chance, of course – but I don't want to see the inside of a French prison again.'

'And so say all of us, sir,' responded the big seaman heartily. 'Once we've got them colours hoisted, we don't strike 'em, not if twenty *Vengeurs* lay us board-and-board!'

Septimus chuckled. 'That sounds as Irish as O'Neill,' he remarked. 'But I'm glad you feel like that. Have you looked through the sloop's armoury?'

'I have, sir – and I've took the liberty of having a dozen pistols ready loaded. The twelve-pounder balls is laid ready in the nettings aside of each gun, there's powder ready to bring on deck, and I've got water-buckets charged and standing by, sir.'

'Very good, Mr Beamish. You locked the powder-magazine, I trust?'

'Yessir. Here's the keys.'

Beamish handed them over and Septimus dropped them into his pocket.

So far as I can find out, these are the only set,' he said in a low voice. 'All the same, you'll keep an eye lifting for any treachery on the part of the French gentleman, Mr Beamish.'

'Aye aye, sir – but I reckon the Monseer's too fond of his life to try and blow us all up.'

'None the less, you'll watch him, Mr Beamish. And if we sight a strange sail he must be taken below and locked in his cabin. Did you find any swords or cutlasses?'

'Cutlasses, sir – a round score of 'em,' answered the seaman. 'In the rack at the bottom of the companionway. They're a various lot, as you might say – all sizes and some of 'em not too sharp.'

'Choose six of the sharpest,' ordered the midshipman, 'and issue one to every man. He's to keep it handy or in his belt. If we go into action I want every man at his station at once, without having to go looking for weapons. And, Mr Beamish, pray choose a light one for me. My wrists aren't steel engines like yours.'

'Aye aye, sir!' grinned Beamish, and hurried below to obey.

Septimus went aft again, and Seaman Eccles came trotting up to him.

'Colours ready for 'oistin', sir!' he reported. ' 'Tain't much of a job, but it's the best we can do.'

'So long as they don't look like the Tricolour they'll do,' nodded Mr Quinn. 'Have them bent on to the halliards.'

As soon as Beamish returned to the deck the five men of the sloop's crew (Frith being at the helm) formed rank and stood to attention while the makeshift British flag was hoisted to the peak of the *Chasseur*'s mainyard. Then the colours were lowered again and the Tricolour bent on ready for hoisting. It might yet be necessary to sail under false colours in order to have a chance of evading recapture.

The sloop swooped onward over the blue like a seabird, her forefoot slicing into the curling seas as she headed ever eastward towards the station of Nelson's blockading fleet. Septimus took a short spell at the helm, relieving Frith so that the seaman could arm himself. He had learned the rudiments of handling a sailing-boat during the few days the *Althea* had spent at Gibraltar, but he grasped the big tiller of this large vessel with some nervousness. Under full sail, however, the *Chasseur* was so perfectly trimmed that she answered to the slightest pressure on the helm, and for a few moments he experienced the real delight of being in full control of a sailing-ship. In a later year, when circumstances placed him in command of a British sloop and 'Quinn of the *Fury*' made himself famous, he was to experience this elation again. On this occasion it was not to last long.

Down in the gloom of a cabin beneath Midshipman Quinn's feet, Lieutenant-de-Vaisseau Brunel was sitting up in his bunk and massaging the wrists of his freed hands. His labours had been rewarded. The cord had parted at last. A light of fanatical determination gleamed in his dark eyes as he leaned forward to wrestle with the cords that bound his feet.

2

Six bells in the forenoon watch – eleven o'clock by landsmen's time – was just past when O'Neill's hail came from the masthead.

'Deck there! Smoke on the horizon, right ahead!'

Septimus shouted an acknowledgement, and then paused to consider. Smoke might mean a burning ship, and that might be the work of the *Althea*. It was safest to steer clear of the smoke. But on the other hand, if the frigate was somewhere near, was it not his duty to rejoin her as soon as possible?

He decided not to alter course for the present. The sloop sped on towards the faint smear of smoke, which was soon visible from the deck. Beamish, at his elbow, suddenly cocked an ear.

'By your leave, sir – aye, there it is again! That's gunfire, sir, sure as I'm a seaman!'

A moment later a slight lull in the following wind enabled the sound to be heard more clearly. Septimus heard it himself this time, the dull pounding of ships' cannon, broadside after broadside.

He turned to speak to the helmsman, and was interrupted by another hail from the masthead.

'Deck there! 'Tis the divil of a fight, sir – I can see the flashes through the smoke!'

'Can you see the vessels?' demanded the midshipman.

'Only the mastheads, sir! Two of thim's at it, anyway!' O'Neill sounded excited. He had an Irishman's delight in a fight.

'Bear up a little and steer for the smoke,' Septimus told Frith, and sprang into the shrouds.

He had the spyglass that had belonged to the *Chasseur*'s captain in his pocket and intended to see for himself. As he clambered hand over fist up the swaying foot-ropes he told himself that the chances were in favour of the *Althea*'s being one of the battling ships. The frigate would be heading for the rendezvous off Toulon today, and the position of the fight could not be more than fifteen miles west of Toulon. If it was the *Vengeur* which was the other ship, the French captain was a daring or reckless man to come so near the waters where Nelson and the English fleet held sway. It was Captain Gruvel of the *Vengeur* who had taken Septimus prisoner, and the midshipman well remembered that thin sallow face and the restless glittering eyes. He was a dangerous adversary on even terms – and the *Althea* would be heavily out-gunned by the French warship.

'Sorra a doubt but the old *Althy*'s yonder, sir,' O'Neill greeted him as he swarmed up the last few feet to the truck of the mast. 'Sure and I'd know the sound of her guns annywhere!'

Septimus hooked an arm round the stay and got his glass to his eye.

'One gun sounds very like another at five miles distance,' he remarked with mild sarcasm, 'but in a few minutes, O'Neill, we shall see.'

The slight but continual dipping and swaying of the tall mast to which he clung made it very difficult to hold the glass steady. The smoke on the horizon, now a considerable cloud, swung into the narrow circle of vision several times, and out of it again almost at once, before Midshipman Quinn was able to make out more than a dun blur on a dancing line of blue. It was a low, spreading cloud, the drifting smoke of gunfire, not the towering smoke of a burning ship. At last he made out the cross-shaped spars of topmasts – certainly there were two three-masted vessels engaged in close conflict, and one of them was considerably larger than the other. From the heart of the smoke cloud came spurts of orange flame. Even above the singing of the breeze in the rigging and the rush of the waves he could hear the continuous *thud-thud-thud* of cannon.

He rested his eye from the spyglass for a moment. When he looked again a slight gap had blown in the smoke, and through it showed, for a moment, the side of a big ship, red-brown with a broad black line along it. Septimus had seen that ship emerging from the mist just before he was captured, and he could not mistake it. That was the 60-gun ship *Vengeur,* and it was a hundred to one that the vessel she was engaged with was the frigate *Althea.* He pocketed his glass.

'Is it into the fun we'll be going, sir?' asked O'Neill eagerly.

'Stay here,' returned the midshipman shortly. 'Report what you see.'

He climbed down the ratlines, weighing in his mind as he descended the question O'Neill had voiced. The sloop was a fairly valuable prize, and he had only six men. The help she would be able to give the frigate in a battle was very small. No one could blame him if he held his course for Toulon, which was what a prudent officer would do. Nevertheless, Mr Quinn's decision had been taken – as he realised – before he left the masthead. He leaped down from the shrouds to the deck and saw the faces of the seamen turned towards him with the same eager expression O'Neill's had worn.

'Where is the Frenchman Cartier?' he demanded.

'Asked leave to go below for his topcoat, sir,' answered Dobbs.

'He should have been escorted,' Septimus said sharply.

The man could do little harm, however, since Brunel's cabin was locked.

'Attention, every man,' he continued rapidly. '*Vengeur* and *Althea* are engaged ahead of us. We're going in, and we shall bear down—'

He was interrupted by the cheer that broke simultaneously from his five listeners. It was echoed by a wild Irish screech from O'Neill at the masthead. Septimus held up his hand for silence.

'We shall bear down from north-east,' he went on, 'heading straight for the Frenchman. There's just a chance she won't see us until we're almost alongside. Frith will bring the sloop up into the wind and lay us board-and-board – I'll want three grapnels prepared, Mr Beamish, to lock us together.'

'Aye aye, sir,' rapped the giant, his eyes agleam.

'That brings our larboard guns against the *Vengeur*'s timbers. They must be loaded and run out, ready. One broadside will be fired. Immediately after it, every man Jack of the sloop's crew will board the *Vengeur*. Is that understood?'

There was a hoarse growl of assent. Beamish stepped forward.

'Begging pardon, sir, but are the two ships grappled?'

'I was unable to see for sure,' admitted Septimus. 'But they're at close quarters, and if the *Vengeur*'s captain is the man I think him, he'll try to board the frigate as soon as he can. I'm relying on his doing so before we reach the fight. We shall then take the French in rear, and may do some good work for our shipmates.'

He turned to glance at the scene of the battle, now little more than two miles away across the sparkling water. Much of the smoke had drifted clear, and the red hull of the French battleship was in full view, with the torn sails and rigging of the frigate seen on its further side. The thunder of the cannonade sounded very loud now, and its smoke was whirled away to the left instead of hanging about the ships.

'Wind's freshening, sir,' said Frith, with a frown at the straining canvas aloft.

O'Neill's yell came on the heels of his words.

'Deck there! Looks to me as if the French are boarding, sir – you can hear the spalpeens screeching!'

The thin high noise of a hundred voices shouting wildly came to the ears of the *Chasseur*'s crew. Septimus whirled round to snap orders.

'Mr Beamish! Load all guns. See that every man has cutlass and pistol. Dobbs and Wallace! Go below, find Monsieur Cartier, and lock him in his cabin. Eccles, water-buckets on deck. Step lively!'

The seamen sprinted to obey orders. Septimus, stationing himself beside the helmsman, shouted to O'Neill to come down from the masthead and then fixed his gaze on the sea-fight ahead.

The *Chasseur* was heeling over before the freshening breeze on her starboard quarter, speeding through the water as if she was eager to join the fray. With every few moments the scene grew in clarity and detail, and it was plain that *Vengeur* and *Althea* were locked in a death-grapple. Septimus never forgot the dramatic scene.

Between the cloudless sky and the deeper blue, ridged with white crests, of the sea, the red flank of the French warship floated motionless, hiding all but the bows of the British frigate's black hull. The *Vengeur*'s foremast was leaning drunkenly backwards, her sails were torn and her rigging lines hung in loose ends from the yards. Evidently the *Althea*'s gunners had not allowed her to come to close quarters without suffering a good deal of damage. Across the water to leeward drifted a spreading cloud of smoke, and above the vessels hung a brownish haze shot with red flashes and brief white puffs of smoke. A confused uproar of shots, yells, and cheers grew louder every second.

The midshipman grasped the hilt of the light cutlass Beamish had found for him, and tried to control the excited thumping of his heart. He was not exactly afraid, but he was far from comfortable. Unless there was a complete lack of order and discipline on board the *Vengeur* someone must have seen the approaching sloop by now. She was flying the Tricolour from her peak, and he would not run up the English colours until he was ready to engage. But that moment would very soon be here. Mr Quinn told himself that these desperate heroics were not at all his line – caution and strategy in warfare were his preferences. Almost without his knowing it, his hand stole to his side-pocket and took out his spectacles. With those firmly perched on his nose he felt more confident.

They were barely a mile from the battling ships now, and he could see the muzzles of cannon peering from the *Vengeur*'s gunports.

'Sir!'

Dobbs ran up to him, his whiskered face red and anxious.

'The Frenchy, Cartier, sir!' he panted. 'He's dead – killed!'

'Who killed him?' snapped the midshipman.

'Dunno, sir. He's lyin' stabbed in the alleyway near the door o' the gunnery store – an' what's more, sir, t'other Frog officer's missin'. Bust open the door of his cabin!'

So Brunel was free and hiding somewhere in the ship. Brunel could be dangerous and must be found at once.

'Get Eccles and Wallace and search the ship!' Septimus rapped. 'Hurry, man!'

Dobbs turned to obey. He had not taken three paces when there was a cry from for'ard, followed by the crack of a pistol. Up from the forehatch sprang a wild figure with gleaming eyes and black locks streaming in the wind. It was Charles Brunel, a smoking pistol in his hand. He looked round him desperately, saw the seamen making at him, and ran for the weather bulwarks. Beamish, drawing his pistol, sprinted to intercept him.

'*Vive la France!*' came the Frenchman's cracked scream as he leapt on to the rail.

Beamish's pistol banged a reply. Brunel flung up his arms and fell forward into the sea, shot through the head.

'Quarters, there!' shouted the midshipman as the seamen crowded to the side to look over. 'We'll be in action in five minutes! Is anyone hurt?' he added as Beamish came running aft.

'No, sir – the Frog loosed off at Wallace and missed.'

'Very good. Man the larboard guns, Mr Beamish, if you please, and stand by to fire and board.'

'Aye aye, sir.'

A bare half-mile of choppy sea separated the sloop from the roar and smoke of the battle. The death of Cartier and Brunel's escape were unimportant matters compared with the fight to come. Mr Quinn, forcing himself to keep cool, ran an eye over his men as they stood to their guns. Only two of the twelve-pounders could be manned, and their crews of two and three men were too small to reload them quickly. One shot, and then up the side of the *Vengeur* – that was all he could do. He managed to grin at the thought of the queer boarding-party they would make. Beamish in his leopard-skin, three of the others in red-and-green motley, himself in black satin Court dress.

There couldn't be more than a quarter of a mile to go now. Still no aggressive action from the French warship. All her attention was concentrated on the struggle with *Althea*, no doubt. He could picture the mad fighting as the frigate's men strove to fling back the superior forces of their opponents from their decks. . . .

What, he wondered suddenly, had Brunel been doing for'ard? Why had he killed Cartier – for he it must have been who stabbed his fellow-countryman? Cartier must have been trying to stop him from doing something. What?

Scarcely had the problem entered his mind when his eye saw the answer. Out of the sloop's forehatch burst a mushroom of oily black smoke. Charles Brunel's last work for his country before he died had been done well. The *Chasseur* was on fire.

3

Beamish had seen the gush of smoke. He darted to the forehatch and disappeared, to appear again almost immediately and race aft to his commander.

'Gunnery store's afire, sir!' he panted. 'It's blazing down there – no getting at it!'

'Better abandon ship, sir,' ventured Frith, behind him at the helm.

Septimus's thoughts raced through his mind. It was a matter of minutes before the fire, fanned by the strong breeze, spread and reached the magazine. To rig and man the pumps was impossible in the time. This, then, was to be the end of his heroics – to abandon his prize, to take to the boat and pull away, to watch the *Chasseur* blown sky-high when the fire had its will—

The smoke and thunder of the sea-fight was a bare four hundred yards ahead when he made the daring decision.

'Mr Beamish!' he cried. 'Two hands to the mainbrace, two to

lower the boat! Larboard your helm, Frith – bring the wind abeam!'

As the sloop swung away from her course, heeling over until the wavetops lopped over her lee rail, he sprang to the flag halyards. Down came the Tricolour, and up soared the English flag. The captured *Chasseur* was to serve Britain after all.

Red flame was shooting from the foredeck now, licking upward at the foot of the sail. Beamish and his men had the larboard boat lowered and its painter made fast to the rail.

'Now the grapnels, Mr Beamish – lash the ends and stand by to launch them at the Frenchman's bows!'

The sloop was almost dead to windward of the locked ships. He could see *Althea*'s stern, and the flash of steel as men fought there. *Vengeur*'s bows were towards him.

'Helm over!' he told Frith. 'Put her before the wind and sheer her alongside!'

Round came the *Chasseur*, her bowsprit pointing straight at the French warship like a fencer's foil. With the wind right astern, she foamed down upon the big ship. Someone aboard *Vengeur* had seen the little craft's charge. A few figures gesticulated from the foredeck, a scattered fire from half-a-dozen muskets crackled ineffectually as, with smoke pouring from her and her foresail ablaze, she rushed to the attack.

'Down mainsail!'

With the red hull of the Frenchman only a pistol-shot away, the mainyard came down with a rush. The blazing sloop ran in under the huge bowsprit and Frith's strong hands pushed the tiller over until her own bowsprit rasped along the enemy's side.

'Away grapnels!' came Beamish's bull roar, and three grapnels hurled through the air on their lines.

Every grapnel caught in the bowsprit rigging of the *Vengeur* and held fast. Although the lowering of the mainsail had taken much of the way off her, the jerk as the sloop was brought up short threw Septimus off his balance. When he recovered himself he saw that the *Chasseur* was held close against the fore part of the bigger vessel's hull, the two wooden sides grinding and splintering as the

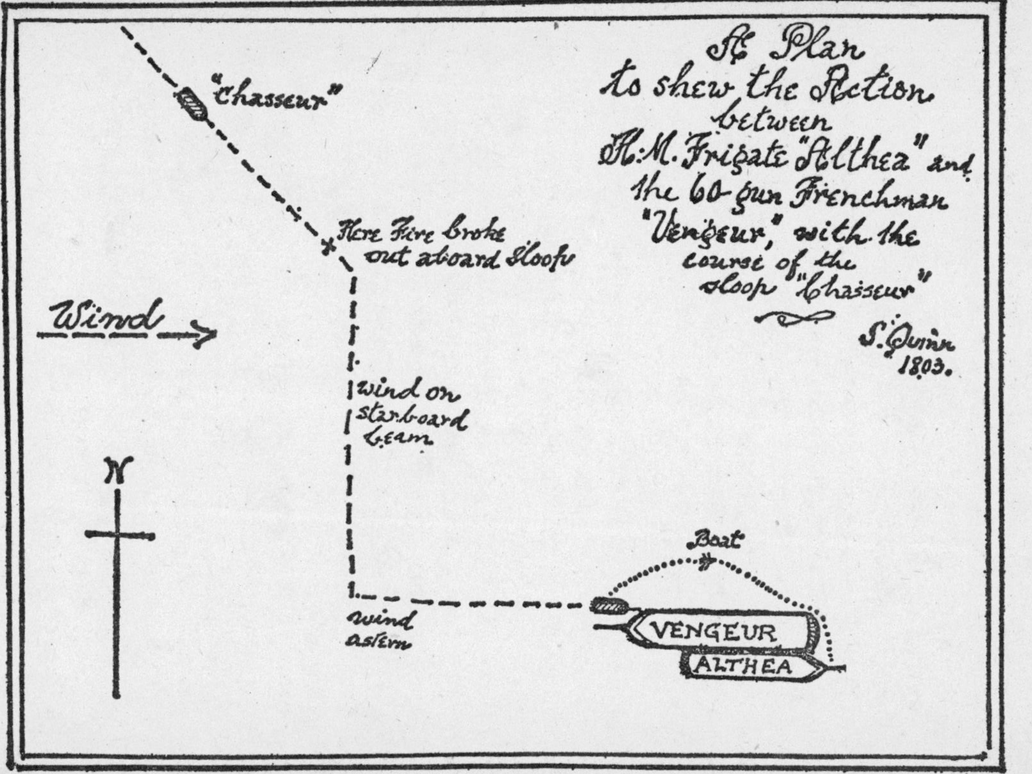

Midshipman Quinn's sketch of the Sea Fight.
From his private Log.

waves set them heaving against each other. The sloop's foresail was a sheet of flame and flames stabbed upwards with orange-red tongues from half-a-dozen places on the deck-planking. It might be five minutes or more, or only five seconds, before the fire reached the magazine and it blew up. That explosion must undoubtedly damage the *Vengeur* severely – but they could not wait for that moment.

'All hands – abandon ship!' shouted the midshipman above the tumult of sound that came from overhead.

Musket-balls sang through the air about him as he started for the bulwarks. A loud groan made him turn. The faithful Frith was sinking to the deck, blood welling from his chest just below the shoulder.

'Overside wi'ye, sir!' he growled almost angrily as Septimus bent over him. 'Ye've not a second to spare – and I'm done!'

'Maybe – but I'm not!' retorted Septimus, and with a great effort he got his shoulder under the man's body and staggered to his feet.

Again the muskets banged and he heard the balls thud into the deck behind him as he tottered towards the rail. Beamish sprang to meet him. Frith was quickly transferred to the giant seaman's shoulders and carried down into the waiting boat. Septimus, the last to leave the vessel he had commanded for less than a day, was not slow to follow. The moment he landed in the boat she was shoved off, and Dobbs and Wallace at the oars sent her flying through the water away from the doomed sloop.

No musket-shots followed them. Midshipman Quinn, twisting round in the sternsheets to look back, saw the reason. The few men available on *Vengeur*'s deck – all the rest were needed to deal with the frigate – were frantically trying to cut away the bowsprit rigging to which the grapnels were attached. They were not having much success. The sloop was wrapped in flame and at any moment she would blow up.

'How is he?' he inquired, turning to Beamish, who was binding a pad of cloth soaked in seawater on Frith's wounded chest.

'He won't die, sir, but he's out of the fight just now.' Beamish stopped his rough bandage-work to stare up at the midshipman. 'What about us, sir?' he added. 'Are we out of the fight too?'

The question brought Septimus back to the realities of their situation. The rapid succession of events, the thrill and tension of the sloop's rush down wind upon the *Vengeur* followed by their present release from danger, had brought an odd lethargy upon him. He summoned all his wits. There was something yet to be done, and he must take command.

What the situation on the *Althea*'s deck was, he could only guess. The continuous din of the fighting gave no hint of its progress, and the big hull of the French warship hid the frigate. Judging by the few men on her decks, *Vengeur* had used the greater part of her crew in boarding the frigate, and that meant that the British seamen would be hard-pressed by forces at least twice as numerous as their own. That they were still fighting was shown by the fact that their colours still fluttered from the yard-arm. The red-white-and-blue flag could just be seen, tattered but defiant, above the smoke and through the tangle of rigging.

'When will *Chasseur*'s magazine blow up?' he muttered impatiently.

Beamish heard him. 'May be a few minutes even now, sir,' he declared. 'Double-skin magazine, that was – iron skin between the timbers.'

A few minutes yet. When the sloop did blow up, she would send up part of the *Vengeur*'s bows too, and probably set her on fire at once. That would disconcert the French boarding-party. Some of them might panic, or the French captain might withdraw a party to deal with the fire. That would be the moment to strike.

He leaned forward suddenly, grasping the boat's tiller and swinging it round.

'Pull, men! Send her along! We've work to do!'

'Praise be – and didn't I know it!' chuckled O'Neill, fingering his cutlass.

The wind had already carried the boat to leeward along the *Chasseur*'s flank. Septimus steered close in under her stern. If any Frenchman was at the rail, he either did not see them or ignored them. A small boat with seven men was not likely to distract attention from the main fight. As they rounded the big red ship, the long bowsprit of the *Althea* came into view, for the two ships were locked bows to stern.

Midshipman Quinn was not acting without his customary forethought. Although he could see nothing of the fierce fighting which was going on aboard the frigate, he knew that the boarders must have made good their footing there. It was therefore very likely that the *Althea*'s men, forced back from the bulwarks, would be defending the quarterdeck end of their ship, where the colours flew. It was Mr Quinn's intention to gain the foredeck and counter-attack from there, taking the French in rear as he had at first planned to do before Charles Brunel provided him with the weapon of a fire-ship.

'Lay to your oars!' he shouted impatiently. 'Easy all! Stand by!'

The boat glided swiftly beneath the stern windows of the Frenchman and the familiar figurehead of their own ship appeared overhead beneath the long bowsprit. He steered beneath the bowsprit, and Beamish, standing up in the boat, got a hand over the sprit-stay as the oarsmen held water. In a second he was up, balancing with a hand on the long 'dolphin-striker' and ready to haul up the others. Frith called faintly after them to wish them luck as one by one they heaved themselves on to the stay.

Such work was child's play to seamen who could climb a rope by using their hands alone, but Septimus found it the hardest bit of that crowded day's work. Had it not been for the steel muscles of Tod Beamish, ever at hand to help him, he would not have managed the climb to the bowsprit. In his ears, as he panted and clung in undignified fashion with the giant seaman's hand gripping his collar, was the ever-growing roar of the fight – an indescribable medley of shouting, screaming, pistol-shots and the grind and clash of steel. When, at last, he crouched on the massive round of the bowsprit just beyond the bows, he could see the frigate's deck and what was happening there.

He had hardly time to realise that the *Althea*'s men were

hemmed in on the quarterdeck, and that the mass of striving men with their backs to him were French sailors, before there was a rending explosion from somewhere in front of him. The bowsprit leaped beneath him like a live thing and the whole ship shuddered with the shock. The sloop had blown up.

Through the acrid smoke that made a thick vapour on the frigate's deck he saw the rank of Frenchmen falter. Some few of them ran back, shouting excitedly and pointing to the column of smoke rising from the foredeck of their ship. This was the moment.

'Come on!' he yelled, and scrambled to his feet.

Regardless now of the drop into the water far below, he leapt across the few feet that separated him from the bulwarks and landed with a flying jump on the deck. After him rushed the five seamen, led by Beamish.

In the wild charge that followed Septimus scarcely noticed that the deck was littered with dead and dying men and slippery with blood. He certainly did not realise that he was still wearing his spectacles. He was cheering madly, and so were his men. They raced for the packed mass of Frenchmen together, and together they flung themselves into the fight.

Midshipman Quinn could never recall, afterwards, the details of that surprise attack. There was a savage face in front of him, a raised pistol. He cut fiercely at it and his blade met flesh and bone. The face disappeared. A man with blood running down his cheek thrust at him with a sword, catching the point in his coat-sleeve. From beside him Beamish's mighty arm swept down and the man fell with a scream. Carried on by the impetus of his rush, slashing and thrusting, he was conscious only of a fierce desire to win through to the *Althea*'s men, to join forces with Barry and Cocker and the rest of his shipmates.

Suddenly he found himself with no opponent in front of him. The after deck was the scene of a dozen man-to-man fights. He caught a glimpse of Captain Sainsbury, some yards on his left, coolly parrying the thrust of a French sword. And then he saw his old enemy Lieutenant Pyke.

Pyke was down on one knee close to the rail, his right arm

dangling helpless and his sword in his left hand, desperately parrying the savage cuts of a French officer who stood over him. Septimus sprang forward with his reddened cutlass raised.

'*Althea!*' he yelled at the full pitch of his lungs – it was the only battle-cry that occurred to him.

The French officer spun on his heel and made a sweeping cut at this new adversary. Septimus ducked beneath it, straightened himself like lightning, and lunged. The point of his cutlass took the Frenchman in the throat, and the man flung up his arms and fell backwards.

At that moment there rose on the air a noise like the growling of a gigantic dog. It was the hoarse cheer of the *Althea*'s men as they surged to the attack. Step by step the Frenchmen gave back along the slippery deck, the heart gone out of them. Most of them had by now realised that their ship was in danger. Uncertainty as to whether they should regain her deck or not, coupled with this unexpected rear attack by a force of extraordinary fighters in strange costumes, had unnerved them. The tide of battle had turned.

The uproar swelled suddenly, French oaths and yells rising above the din. For the *Vengeur*, her decks alive with flickering flames, was drifting slowly away from the frigate. Beamish and his men had severed the grappling-ropes.

After that it was easy to deal with the Frenchmen who had been left on board the *Althea*. Many of them lost their lives in trying to leap across the widening space between the two ships, others flung down their arms. Among those remaining on the deck of the British vessel was the French captain, the sallow-faced Gruvel, who fought on like a madman until a pair of grinning seamen tripped him up and sat on him, refusing to let him get up until he promised to surrender his sword to Captain Sainsbury like a good Monseer.

As for the doomed *Vengeur*, nothing could be done to save her. The frigate, severely damaged in the battle and holed below the waterline, was powerless to help. Slowly the great ship drifted away, the flames licking higher and higher about her masts and lower rigging. The victors watched her turn as some gallant soul on board strove to get her under control. Slowly the blazing ship heeled before the wind and began to move through the water. Then, with blinding suddenness, she seemed to dissolve in an immense fountain of fire. The flames had reached her powder-magazine.

4

In the lantern-lit stern cabin of the frigate *Althea* Captain Sainsbury sat at the head of the table. His thin face was rendered even grimmer than usual by reason of a long strip of sticking-plaster running from nose to ear. Some of the grimness was no doubt due to the fact that thirty seamen had been killed and three officers and forty-two men wounded in the sea-fight with the *Vengeur,* while his ship was so badly damaged that she would take another day to reach Lord Nelson's fleet off Toulon. The decks had been cleared and the jury mizzen-topmast rigged, but the ceaseless clanking of the pumps told of the serious damage to her hull.

His expression changed to something like satisfaction as he glanced round the dozen or so men who were his guests that night at dinner. There was some reason for that satisfaction. The *Althea* had completed her mission and had acquired most valuable information about the French coastal defences, and – more spectacular success – she had fought and sunk a 60-gun French warship, a feat which was almost without parallel in naval history and which would make the *Althea* famous throughout the navy. He felt almost sorry for his chief guest and prisoner, Captain Gruvel of the *Vengeur,* who sat sullenly at his right hand.

Captain Sainsbury very rarely smiled, but a smile of pleasure crept across his face as his glance fell upon the two officers who sat opposite him. One was his First Lieutenant, red-faced George Pyke. The other was a small midshipman with a grave face. Both had their right arms in slings.

Mr Midshipman Quinn had not realised that a French

sword-thrust had bitten deeply into his forearm until the fight was over. He had not expected to be invited to dine in the captain's cabin, and thought it must be because he was better able to represent the midshipman's berth than either Charles Barry or Fitzroy Cocker, who had both been slightly wounded in the hand-to-hand fighting. He had been somewhat embarrassed when Lieutenant Pyke, as he entered the cabin, had extended his left hand and barked at him – 'Hah! Saved my life, Mr Quinn! Deucedly obliged, sir!' – and still more so when he listened to Captain Sainsbury's brief commendation of his conduct.

At the moment he was feeling uncomfortable, for the glittering eyes of the French captain, who was sitting opposite him, were fixed upon him angrily. Gruvel turned suddenly away from him to wave a finger under the nose of Captain Sainsbury.

'I tell you zis, *mon capitaine!*' he vociferated in explosive English. 'My ship, she would not 'ave been beaten only for zis – zis boy who sit 'ere!'

He took the finger away to jab it towards Septimus.

'That, Monsieur,' responded Captain Sainsbury calmly, 'is exactly what I have said in my report to Lord Nelson.'

'And that being so, Captain Gruvel and gentlemen,' barked Lieutenant Pyke unexpectedly, rising to his feet glass in hand, 'I'll ask you all to rise and drink a toast. Hah! To Mr Midshipman Quinn!'

The toast was drunk with acclamation. As for Mr Midshipman Quinn, he was scarlet in the face. So great was his confusion that he began to fumble in his pocket. Not until the chuckles broke out round the captain's table did he realise what he had done. He had put on his spectacles.

We hope you have enjoyed this Beaver Book. Here are some of the other titles:

A Knight and his Castle What it was like to live in a castle, by R. Ewart Oakeshott

The Last of the Vikings Henry Treece's exciting story, in the saga tradition, about the young Harald Hardrada, King of Norway; with superb illustrations by Charles Keeping

Beyond the Wide World's End Set in 1810, this is the story of how Timothy, Jane and Brandy the dog journey across Ireland in search of Timothy's dead mother's family; by Meta Mayne Reid

Coral Wreck A mysterious scroll with clues which lead to a sunken Spanish treasure ship provides hero Dirk Rogers with exciting and sometimes dangerous adventures in the South Seas

The Glass Knife Gripping and intriguing story about a boy who has been reared to become a human sacrifice. Set in South America before the European discovery of the New World; illustrated by Victor Ambrus

The Twelve Labours of Hercules The adventures of the hero Hercules, beautifully retold by Robert Newman; illustrated superbly by Charles Keeping

New Beavers are published every month and if you would like the *Beaver Bulletin* – which gives all the details – please send a stamped addressed envelope to:

Beaver Bulletin
The Hamlyn Group
Astronaut House
Feltham
Middlesex TW14 9AR